Mindfulness
...as a Second Language®

A No-Nonsense Guidebook for Creating
a Lasting, Fulfilling Meditation Practice

Nicholas Stein, CMT-P

Foreword by Valerie Alexander

Mindfulness as a Second Language

Copyright © 2020 by Valerie Alexander and Nicholas Stein

Published by
Goalkeeper Media
www.Goalkeeper.net

This book is available in print and as an eBook.

Author Photo of Nicholas Stein by Michael Lewis
Author Photo of Valerie Alexander by Vivian Lin
Cover Layout by Miurel Castillo
Interior Design by Ramesh Kumar Pitchai

ISBN-13: 979-8561794711
ISBN-10: 8561794711

TABLE OF CONTENTS

FOREWORD

By Valerie Alexander

Near the end of 2016, I started a tech company. Before going too far down that road, let me say up front, it didn't survive. But some amazing things came from the experience, and one of the best was meeting Nick Stein.

Nick and I were part of the same large, Meetup group in Pasadena, California. It met early Friday mornings and had a weekly speaker, which was me in July of 2017, talking about women in the tech startup world, and was Nick in January of 2018, talking about bringing mindfulness into your company as a strategic business advantage.

Usually I would hear the speaker, network a little with other attendees and leave, but something about Nick, and how accessible he made the idea of meditation (a topic I had been telling myself I needed to re-visit), compelled me to go stand in the large crowd of people waiting to speak with him. It also could have been that he, like me, was a veteran of the entertainment industry, now moved on to more rewarding pursuits, and that made me curious.

I honestly can't recall the specifics of that conversation, but I remember that we exchanged cards, and the next day, I got an email from him recommending the book, *Why Buddhism is True* by Robert Wright. I immediately added it to my audiobook queue, listened and reached out, wanting to discuss it further. That's when Nick, much to my surprise, invited me to join his small, private monthly meditation group – a group that had been together for years. Out of everyone at that Friday morning meetup, I was the only one invited into this inner circle. Must have been fate.

Despite being insanely busy, I carved the date in my calendar, excited to avail myself of Nick's mindfulness teachings. Unfortunately, this group conflicted almost every month with another monthly event that I had to go to for my struggling startup, but on the few dates that didn't overlap, I made a point to be there. By the second session, I was hooked.

Not only was this the first time a meditation practice resonated with me, but the way Nick gave us permission to experience it in whatever way served us, without ever feeling like we were failing, made me want to go back over and over.

After the third session, I hung around to talk to my new mindfulness guru. We walked out on the sidewalk in front of the meditation center in Studio City, California, said our good-byes to the others, and I asked Nick if he thought he had a book in him. He shared that he didn't think so, but others kept telling him to write one anyway. I told him we had a lot to talk about.

As the publisher of the series, and the holder of the U.S. Registered Trademark on the phrase, *"…as a Second Language"* for self-help and personal growth books, I am always on the lookout for just the right person to share much-needed guidance. The tricky part of this series is getting the right tone. I've actually released as many authors from their contracts as published because of how hard it is to convey one's vast knowledge about a subject while still making it feel like a good friend offering sage advice in a non-judgmental, easily accessible way.

Elisabeth Stitt managed to do it perfectly in writing about joyful parenting. Stacy Parker's gentle voice takes people through their grief with grace and beauty, and Nancy Pia's creativity leaps off the page. It takes a special gift to create something so useful with such authority without it sounding like a lecture or an instruction manual.

The following week, Nick and I had lunch. We outlined what a book called *Mindfulness as a Second Language* would look like, and he was in. A few days later, he sent me the essay, "Why I Meditate," and I knew instantly that this was going to be another spectacular addition to the *"…as a Second Language"* series. I also knew I was reading the introduction to his book.

It's truly been a joy working with Nick, and I am so proud to be the editor and publisher of this work. Throughout, you will find yourself smiling, growing and finding levels of peace, awareness and stillness beyond your expectations. That's certainly been my experience, and it's been amazing.

So with that, I turn it over to my teacher, my dear friend, and the newest incredible writer to join the astounding "*…as a Second Language*" author club, Nick Stein.

I dedicate this book to my beloved sister Katry,
who left us way too soon.

INTRODUCTION
WHY I WROTE THIS BOOK

For much of my 60 plus years I've been ruled by an unruly mind. It, in turn, seemed governed by a disorderly and unreliable world. I habitually deemed myself a victim of circumstances, what I now call a "situational neurotic." If things were good, I was happy; if things were not so good, I could get nervous, depressed, anxious or just downright unpleasant to be around.

Despite this internal struggle I was seen as high functioning by most.

Married to a great woman, I had a very respectable free-lance career in non-fiction TV production, hailed from a big and interesting family, had lots of friends, so seemed to have it all.

But that persona was a two-dimensional cardboard cutout of the real me. Inside, I was, too often, a hot mess. My drive to be a "player" in the entertainment industry, to always be seen as a successful producer, left me terrified to be between jobs. When I was between jobs, instead of enjoying some well deserved downtime, I'd go into my "get a gig" mode and worry away my unpaid vacation. I was distracted by shiny objects and made anxious by perceived threats. I was completely lost in my head and didn't even know I was lost.

There is a familiar adage in neuropsychology about how our brain cells communicate with one another. The saying goes, "What fires together wires together." In other words, the more negative the thoughts, the stronger the neural pathways become and the more difficult it becomes to stop them. This is why our obsessive thoughts that cause depression, anxiety, panic and obsession can become so difficult to combat.

This would explain why my life-long cultivation of apprehension had shrunk my comfort zone to a place where good times were short and bad times lingered; where positive thoughts slid away like Teflon and negative ones stuck like Velcro. Like many, I mistakenly thought that temporary conditions were permanent and permanent conditions were real.

Overreacting became my default mode with hyper-reactivity my go-to defense against any perceived crisis. Looking back, it seems I was always putting out birthday candles with a fire hose. It was exhausting for me and exasperating to my wife.

In a heartbeat, triggered by a minor domestic squabble, an important email not returned, evidence of a personal mistake (no matter how minor), or even a snarky text without a smiley face (God forbid), I would start to worry, project and even catastrophize. In response to these cascading thoughts, I would freeze, fight or flee, all the while over-thinking to try and "fix" the problem.

Desperate to get off this emotional merry-go-round, and yet, once again, caught up in the latest "career crisis," I was guided by a wise counselor towards mindfulness and meditation. As I read books on the topic, meditated and studied other material, I finally came face to face with my inner landscape – a vast place I didn't even know was there.

By intentionally being still and going within, unexpected insights arose resulting in a surprising measure of peace over my unruly mind. By committing to a daily practice of sitting, and by recognizing that the incessant voice in my head was simply a sign of my human condition, I began to feel I'd been handed the owner's manual to my mind.

The basic instructions seemed easy enough: sit, breathe and pay attention to the present moment, and yet, as any meditator will tell you, it was shockingly difficult at first. It's like learning to read braille. You literately have to feel it to understand it.

Over time, as the concepts of mindfulness began to merge with my experience of meditation, my practice began to profoundly change how I thought about how I thought.

By allowing the normal traffic of ideas, opinions, plans and worries to simply come and go, by having a genuine intention to drop my "story" and be present; by using the anchor of the breath (and other concentration techniques) to come back to the now, I learned how to encourage my mental processes to slow down to a point where I could actually hang out in the gaps between my thoughts.

And there it was, even if just for a moment: a wakeful peace for my heretofore-unmanageable mind. The more I practiced, the more I could see the impermanence, non-importance and even fecklessness of so many of my thoughts. As I began to understand this truth, I almost magically started to suffer less. By learning to meditate, I was fundamentally changing my relationship with my cognitive process, and this realization changed my responses to the tumult of life.

It's a dreadful cliché but true: you do have to hit rock bottom before being open to something new. My painful psychological crisis became the catalyst for my meditation practice; a daily act of self-care that enriches and protects me every day.

It's been a long road that's brought me to this place – a place where I could write a book about how mindful meditation saved my life and how it restores me. I hope that what I've learned along the way will help you navigate the vagaries of whatever challenges life throws at you.

For me, meditation is a daily discipline, but it is not a destination. I don't meditate to try and become peaceful, I become more peaceful because I meditate. And it's called a practice because that's what it is. We practice mindfulness when we're meditating so we can be more mindful when we aren't.

Just wait.
You'll see.
And it will be wonderful.

CHAPTER 1

My Rough Road to Mindfulness

I remember it was a Monday. It was dawn and it was cold, even for the Texas border with New Mexico. Together six of us blazed across the early morning sky in a Sikorsky UH-60 Black Hawk. Large, loud, and fast, the nickname for this four-bladed, twin-engine helicopter was the Beast.

Moving in excess of 170 mph, the city of El Paso retreated behind us as the slums of Juarez stretched out to our left. We were fast and low above the New Mexico desert when my cameraman, Tony, gestured to me and to Kevin, the sound engineer, to zip up our coats and pull down our caps. I grinned at both of them as if to say, "Well, here we go again, boys!"

Our U.S. Customs and Border Protection (CBP) crew consisted of a pilot, co-pilot and a well-armed Aviation Enforcement Agent named Oscar. They all wore the visored helmets and the tan flight suits identifying them as members of CBP's elite Air and Marine Operations. It was so loud inside the Beast that our internal *comms* were conducted via heavy-duty headphones wired within the fuselage; that's how we were briefed on our mission.

We were heading east across the state to the New Mexico-Arizona border to support a dozen Border Patrol agents already on the ground. They were in pursuit of a large group of bodies (Border Patrol's rather cynical slang for people crossing the border) who were heading north. Their movement had been detected by electronic *hits* emanating from underground seismic sensors that special agents had set along known trails. Despite this technological advantage, the ground agents were having a hard time finding the group in this vast wilderness.

The helicopter crew's mission was twofold: (a) to be their eye in the sky, and (b) to transport them from ridge to ridge, hopscotching some agents ahead of others as they *cut sign* on the ground.

Sign is any physical evidence of disturbance in the environment left behind by animals or humans. The detection of this *sign* is called *sign cutting*. Many people think that human tracking is just following footprints, but trained trackers look for much more. They look for kicked-over rocks, soil depressions, clothing fibers, changes in vegetation, ambient noise or lack thereof, etc. The tracker looks for any disturbance – the *sign* – left behind by the person or persons being tracked.

As usual, we had no idea who we were chasing. The choices were (a) migrants coming to the U.S. in pursuit of a better life, or (b) cartel drug mules, possibly armed, bringing narcotics into the country. We hoped for the former and were prepared for the latter.

Now, let me hit pause in this story to ask what may be your most obvious question right now: how is it possible that a book entitled *Mindfulness as a Second Language* could begin inside a Black Hawk helicopter shrieking along the U.S.-Mexican border? Good question.

Like many others, I arrived at my meditation practice via a hard road driven by deep suffering. In the spring and summer of 2012, I was in trouble. A serious dose of depression, anxiety and anger had helped me dig a big hole for myself, and I was still digging.

In the pages ahead, I will explain how my unplanned journey to practice, study, teach, train, speak and write about mindfulness came directly from the stress I experienced while producing the cable TV series *Border Wars* for the National Geographic Channel. I'll share all the unpleasant details soon enough, but first, let's get back to the events of that cold Monday at the border in 2011.

By 5:00 pm, we'd been on this mission all day and the terrain had grown increasingly rugged. Picking up and deploying agents was getting tougher each time as we inched closer to running out of both fuel and daylight. Soon we'd have to return to El Paso with no results: no apprehensions for the CBP agents and no story for our TV series.

We were flying above the rim of a heretofore hidden box canyon when Oscar spotted movement in the heavy brush below. There they were, about 20 men and women scrambling down the steep sides of the canyon, hiding in the mesquite from the Beast. As had happened so many times while making *Border Wars*, my adrenaline spiked while my heart ached as it became clear that these were not drug mules, just frightened refugees from Mexico or Central America.

As the Border Patrol agents closed in on their targets, I asked if we could move the Black Hawk in closer so Tony could film out the side-door and capture the action. Mitch, the pilot, assured me that this maneuver was okay, but he was wrong.

As soon as we moved into position near the canyon wall and began to hover, all hell broke loose. Inexplicably, the entire Black Hawk began to spin like a top. We were turning dizzyingly while dropping precipitously. From my side of the chopper all I could see were canyon walls flying by in a gray blur. This is what I thought: this bird is going down, we're out of control, we're spinning inside a canyon, we're going to hit a wall, or the canyon floor, and we'll burst into flames and die.

Now, the fact that you're reading these words tells you right away (spoiler alert!) that we didn't die that day. Nor did we die the day our Border Patrol vehicle rammed headfirst into a smuggler's truck full of drugs. We also didn't die while filming the dramatic rescue of a cartel drug scout who'd been shot at from a Mexican military helicopter while driving a jet ski in the Rio Grande River. For good measure, we likewise didn't die while crawling through a narrow and shabbily built cartel drug tunnel beneath the streets of Nogales, or when armed bandits (unaffiliated rogue outlaws who preyed on drug mules and migrants alike) tried to scare us by shooting over our heads at 2:00 a.m. one night.

So yes, I am alive to tell these stories because I did not die while making *Border Wars*, but later, sadly, after we'd wrapped production, there were days when I wanted to.

Burn Out

To put it plainly, after three-plus years of producing *Border Wars,* I was exhausted. My schedule was this: my crews and I would spend five to six weeks filming in places like Laredo, El Paso, Nogales, San Diego and even San Juan, Puerto Rico. Once wrapped, I'd have maybe two weeks at home with my wife; then a week in New York, where we edited the show, before heading down to Washington, DC to work with the brass at both National Geographic and the federal agencies we were partnered with. I ran this circuit for almost four years, but my burnout didn't come just from long stretches on the road; it was also the result of unforeseen tectonic shifts at the National Geographic Channel.

Today, when I give the keynote talk, *Border Wars: From Mayhem to Mindfulness,* I tell my audience that you don't have to jump out of a Black Hawk helicopter to get into trouble at work. Any one of us can succumb to the pressures, politics and personalities in a normal office environment. Just when you think your job is safe and your ideas are valued, a single email can lay you low. A company curveball can leave you distressed, even devastated, while sitting in your cubicle. I wrote this book to offer you the same time-tested tools I use to enrich my everyday life and navigate these unavoidable and painful tempests.

Secondary Trauma

For me, being an eyewitness to the unrelenting misery at the U.S.-Mexican border resulted in what's called secondary trauma. This happens when you're exposed, over time, to people who've been marginalized, brutalized and traumatized. As I saw their condition and listened to their detailed descriptions of unthinkable cruelty and suffering, it affected me in ways I didn't understand at the time. Only later did I learn about secondary trauma, and I checked all the boxes.

Even as we chronicled this unremitting wave of human misery, my crews and I were also turning into serious adrenaline junkies. Nearly every day we were involved in some kind of high-speed pursuit, be it by foot, ATV, patrol boat or police vehicle. At first, when chasing a drug-laden van at 90 miles per hour through a small border town, your heart is pumping with fear. With time, however, it becomes the new normal; that's how much we trusted the agents and officers with our lives.

Experiencing all of this with a remarkable crew of fearless filmmakers was a huge part of the high. Natalia, Tony, Kevin, Jon, Barry, Steve; these were just some of the team that risked their lives to capture unprecedented scenes. As episodes began piling up, we became a true *Border Wars* family, working and playing, day and night, right on the edge. This bond made it increasingly difficult to return to our civilian lives and our real families.

Much like soldiers home from war, although hardly an equivalent experience to theirs, we sought out each other's company, even back in Los Angeles. We did this despite being together, nonstop, on the road. As the weeks, months, and years went by, it got harder and harder to relate to almost anyone who wasn't living this frightening and exhilarating life.

The bottom line for my real family was this: I was away from home, in one form or another, about 70% of the time for four straight years. Needless to say, it took a very heavy toll on my marriage. Not at first, but increasingly as ratings remained high and the demand for more episodes persisted.

I was well on my way to a serious personal crisis when, as I mentioned earlier, something wholly unexpected happened back at Nat Geo headquarters.

Nat Geo Upside Down

Some background: I worked for National Geographic Television (NGT) while making *Border Wars*. NGT was the internal production unit that provided programs for the National Geographic Channel (NGC).

One day, while working in South Texas, we were deluged by a storm of frantic emails from our colleagues back in DC and New York. The entire editorial division at NGC had been taken over by a team from Rupert Murdoch's 21st Century Fox.

Some more background: Fox had been NGC's investment and business partner for over 12 years, but there had always been a strong firewall between the corporate and journalistic operations. Fox ran financing, marketing, ad sales and distribution, while National Geographic ran editorial, providing their celebrated programming expertise.

Unknown to almost everyone at NGC, Fox had decided that the channel's ratings and revenues, while good, were just not good enough. Then, as the majority owner, they exercised the nuclear option of the contract to knock down the firewall almost overnight. What happened next was equal parts distressing and disorienting.

Our closest friends, colleagues and bosses back at headquarters began to get fired left and right. Most of them were brilliant and dedicated veterans of the original National Geographic's mission which, since its founding in 1888, was created for "the increase and diffusion of geographic knowledge." It was unfathomable to us that Fox was going to dictate to a division of National Geographic what to write, film, print or air.

Top executives and executive producers, middle management and HR, field producers, writers and directors, even marketing and graphics people were canned. It seemed that the longer your tenure at 17th and M Street, the faster you were pinked-slipped.

While this was coming down, my *Border Wars* family and I were two time zones away in the Rio Grande Valley, South Texas. As we got closer to wrapping production on that slate of shows (we were now up to 50 episodes), my thought was this: we'd finish shooting and editing the current season and then, no doubt, we'd be cancelled by our new Fox overlords.

For me it would be with few regrets. It had been a hell of a run and, as a lifelong freelancer, I would simply go out and find another job. This was not to be.

When I came home for Thanksgiving, I got the startling word that the newly installed NGC president had declared his love for *Border Wars* and was going to renew the series for yet another season; ten more episodes. I thought, "Okay, at least my crews and the team in New York still have their jobs," and so, I figured, we'd just soldier on.

Then in early December, back in DC, I was crossing 17th Street in the pouring rain, sharing an umbrella with the super talented and kind TV executive who'd hired me three plus years earlier. It came down to her to give me the *really* bad news: yes, the series had been renewed for another season, but the new president had also decided to replace me as the showrunner of *Border Wars*.

Shocked and taken aback, I was trying to make sense of what she was telling me. Then, with great emotion in her voice, she went on. It seemed that despite all of our personal sacrifices, critical success and high ratings, this youthful new president (best known for making network reality shows in Hollywood) was sure he could make *Border Wars* better. The next thing I heard was that he'd already chosen my replacement, a hot shot young producer twenty years my junior. In rapid succession I was informed that my brilliant head writer who oversaw all of our post-production in NYC had been fired, and yet somehow I still had a job. It gets worse.

My new job was to take this young producer down to the border and introduce him to all the key people I had established strong relationships with in federal law enforcement.

We're talking about Border Patrol Sector Chiefs all the way down to rank and file line agents, plus Port Officer brass down to the men and women manning the 50 legal land ports of entry from Brownsville, Texas to San Diego, California. I was to vouch for this guy with DEA and ICE agents as well as local police and sheriff departments. Finally, I was to introduce him to the groups that no one had ever filmed with before; Special Ops units like SWAT, BORTAC and BORSTAR.

And oh, along the way, could I please teach him how to do my job.

To say this was an ego-crushing experience is an understatement. I felt utterly betrayed by an organization I had worked for, on and off, since the pilot of Explorer in 1985. It didn't take a genius to figure out that I was now *temporarily* indispensable, but would soon become *especially* dispensable once my tutoring was complete. My big attempt to quit, having written a rather righteous letter of resignation, failed when the Chief Liaison Executive for Public Affairs at the U.S. Customs and Border Protection indicated that his office might not participate in future shows if I wasn't part of the Nat Geo team. It was not surprising to hear them say that. For almost four years my crews and I *were* their comfort zone; in fact, our presence was sought after in every sector along the border.

It took three months to resolve this situation after that young producer was reassigned. Even the Fox people could see that we were, to put it mildly, incompatible. By March of 2012, he was replaced by a more seasoned producer. Thinking I could work with this more mature filmmaker, I reluctantly agreed to return to Texas, knowing that my leaving would cause forty staffers to be out of work.

Fast forward through the next ten dreadful months (I will spare you the really bad parts), and by the time the final season of *Border Wars* was mercifully over, I was a hot mess. I was melting down, stewing in depression and anxiety. I was convinced that my career was shot, and my marriage over. Then, as fate would have it, my beloved father died at the age of 93. I was not in good shape when I joined my siblings in Baltimore for the cremation.

Mindfulness vs. Suffering

So again you're probably asking, what does all of this have to do with mindfulness? The quick answer is this: we are all wired the same way; it's our legacy from 200,000 years ago. That's when our ancient ancestors' brains evolved to resemble the ones we carry around today. Fear, rage and anxiety. Love, joy and compassion; all of our emotions had enormously practical roots when first developed in nomadic, hunter-gatherer groups in the plains of Africa. In other words, my suffering is just a different version of your suffering and vice-versa.

Automatic emotions helped our kin rapidly discern between good and bad, poisonous and safe, friend and foe. Without that hard-wiring, they would not have survived to pass down our genetic materials to future generations.

Today, many of these automatic reactions to our environment have outlived their utility. We now see life-imperiling threats in a knock on the door, an ill-advised tone of voice, or an unwelcome email. Intense worry and anxiety – which are at epic levels today – trigger a myriad of physical responses, including sending one's adrenaline and cortisol levels soaring. The body doesn't lie.

As you'll read, we're not nearly as in control of our thoughts, moods and emotions as we think we are, and there are precious few tools available to help self-regulate and mitigate our suffering. Mindfulness and meditation are two such tools and, working together, they can make all the difference.

Ironically, we've known about them for thousands of years. As you'll learn in these pages, the mindfulness journey we're about to embark on, while presented in a secular and non-religious manner, nevertheless has its roots in Buddhism. It's the Buddhists that famously remind us that all human beings inherently suffer. I know people think this sounds like a downer but it's not. It's a reality check.

The Buddha described suffering in two ways. With a capitol "S" it refers to ruinous injury, disease, torture, and death. With a small "s" it refers to annoyance, inconvenience, frustration, and discomfort. The Buddhists call this everyday disquiet *dukkha,* and it's commonly translated into English as unhappiness or "unsatisfactoriness." As you'll soon appreciate, this concept refers to our nearly constant state of restlessness as we navigate our world. It's the small things (relatively speaking) that take us out of our narrow comfort zones.

All humans seek what's called homeostasis: a state of relative equilibrium where we feel okay and in balance. Ever notice how fleeting these moments are? Once we actually think we feel good, soon we'll *want* something we don't have, or *have* something we don't want. Caught between these poles of desire and aversion, our minds easily convince us that we never have what we *really* want. As a result, we use our magnificent brains – perhaps the most complex phenomena in the universe – to obsessively wish that things could be different from the way they are.

The result is that we employ this glorious instrument in service to the inconsequential as we seek out conditions for our maximum comfort. We are also hyper vigilant to anything that might diminish the chances for our hoped-for ease. Think about it; we're so busy running around creating conditions for our future happiness that we're rarely aware, or grateful, to be living in the only moment we actually ever have: this one.

What to Do?

It's easy to talk about the shortcomings of having a glitchy human brain, but is there anything we can do about it? What could possibly be the antidote to this gnawing sense of lack? How do we regulate our racing minds and runaway emotions? Add to that, how can we help our brains cope with the overwhelming blizzard of data coming at us through our computers, smartphones and other digital devices? Texts, emails, websites, social media; they are almost the air we breathe.

So the question is: is there a method, training, or practice that's especially designed to reduce this level of hard-wired psychosis? Can we mitigate this distress to any degree? Can we find the calm eye of the hurricane? Yes!

Does it have anything to do with mindfulness and meditation? Yes again!

At the end of the day, the best treatment I've found for my suffering and distress boils down to one very simple word: *stillness*. As you'll discover in the chapters ahead, stillness is at the heart of meditation, and meditation is at the heart of mindfulness.

Fast Forward

Back when my life and my TV series were falling apart (and I clearly saw no distinction between the two), I felt like the ultimate victim, but today I understand that I'd begun sowing the seeds of my own downfall long before Fox came onto the scene.

These were the three areas of my greatest peril: (a) I wildly over-identified with my job, (b) when I was home, I wasn't really home, which is to say, I was not present for the needs and concerns of my wife, and finally (c) I had no *inner* life to speak of. In fact I was so clueless that I didn't even know I didn't have one. The bottom line was this: when my job (aka my identity) was taken from me, I had no Self to fall back on.

To wrap up the story of my journey, let me condense the last eight years into a couple of paragraphs.

Three months prior I had received a surprise phone call from an unexpected source. We were filming the aftermath of a successful undercover police raid on a major heroin dealer's house in Laredo when a young woman from a Montreal-based production company called to ask me if I was interested in coming to Canada to work for six months. They said they'd include housing. I said yes.

So by late 2012, I was living in Montreal, in bad shape, and ready to try almost anything to relieve my suffering. I was still working with a therapist back in LA via Skype who suggested meditation as a possible outlet for me. As you'll read later, this was not the first time meditation had come into my awareness, but this time I was ready. I was motivated and, thank goodness, had the right guides to get started.

Mindfulness came to me as secular, science-based and sensible. This time around I had nothing to lose. I committed to meditating every day for a week and when the week was up, I knew something had shifted. It was subtle but it was there. My mental state was stabilizing.

After four years of producing *Border Wars*, my road from burned-out TV producer to meditation practitioner to mindfulness facilitator really kicked in when I came home from Montreal and began studying at UCLA's Mindful Awareness Research Center (MARC). Two years later, I went to the Engaged Mindfulness Institute (EMI) in Massachusetts, where I received a Certification of Mindfulness Facilitation. I was later accepted into the

International Mindfulness Teachers Association (IMTA) and could then officially call myself a mindfulness teacher.

Today, with forty years of TV production in my rear-view mirror, I work, teach and train in a variety of settings, including corporate, private and academic, but a large percentage of my work is still with law enforcement. I have traveled far and wide to bring mindfulness training to U.S. Border Patrol agents and CBP's Port Officers, as well as local police departments from California to Boston.

Exercises

The book you are holding includes three different types of content:

- The main offering will, of course, be about the practice of meditation and mindfulness; what these words mean, their relationship to each other, and the techniques needed to bring them onboard.
- The second area will be stories from my crazy life (before and after starting my practice) and the lives of students I've worked with, that I hope will illustrate certain points about *your* crazy life and how the practice can mitigate your suffering.
- The third part consists of interactive exercises for you to do. These exercises, done in order, will ease you into your mindfulness practice.

EXERCISE: THE RAISIN EXPERIMENT

What are we doing? – Eating a single raisin as a form of attention training. This deliberate act of concentration compels us to be present as we become acutely aware of a level of detail that we typically never notice.

Why? – Mindfully eating a raisin can quickly demystify the concept of mindfulness. As you do this practice, turn off the phone, put aside all distractions and focus your clear awareness on each aspect of the experience. Read about it first and then do the practice. If you don't have a raisin in your vicinity, put the book down and make a commitment to get one in the next 24 hours. Think of this as the best present you can buy yourself this week.

Time Required – Five minutes for this first exercise and then later, try bringing this level of mindfulness to another eating moment, perhaps when you eat an apple or drink a cup of coffee. Mindful eating is a whole area of practice you'll want to explore.

Materials Required – A single raisin.

Start with your raisin:

1. **Holding:** First, take the raisin and hold it in the palm of your hand or between your finger and thumb. Feel its weight, its mass.

2. **Seeing:** Take time to really focus on it; gaze at the raisin with care and full attention. Hold it up to the light. Imagine that you've just dropped in from Mars and have never seen an object like this before in your life. Let your eyes explore every part of it, examining the highlights where the light reflects, the darker hollows, the folds and ridges and any irregularities or unique features.

3. **Touching:** Turn the raisin over between your fingers, exploring its texture. Maybe do this with your eyes closed if that enhances your sense of touch.

4. **Smelling:** Hold the raisin beneath your nose. With each inhalation, take in any smell that emanates from this raisin. As you do this, notice anything interesting that may be happening in your mouth or stomach. Check to see if any memories arise.

5. **Placing:** Slowly bring the raisin up to your lips, noticing how your hand and arm know exactly where to position it. Gently place the raisin in your mouth; without chewing, noticing how it gets into your mouth in the first place. Spend a few moments focusing on the sensations of having it in your mouth and exploring it with your tongue.

6. **Tasting:** When you are ready, bite down on the raisin and notice the waves of sweetness that come from it; a rush of raisin-ness like you've never had before. Without swallowing yet, observe the bare sensations of taste and texture in your mouth and how these change over time, moment by moment.

7. **Swallowing:** When you feel ready to swallow the raisin, see if you can first detect the intention to swallow as it occurs, so that even this intention to eat is experienced consciously before you actually swallow the raisin.

8. **Finally**, see if you can sense what is left of the raisin moving down into your stomach, and feel how your body responds after you have completed this exercise.

Congratulations! Chances are that you invested more time, care and thoughtfulness eating that single raisin than you might have done with a five-course meal at a fancy restaurant.

So now your journey has begun. You're entering a brave new world of intention, attention, focus and concentration, and along the way you'll learn how to generate more calm, more peace and a sense of well-being. We are going in deep and letting go completely – all at the same time. Trust me, you'll enjoy the ride.

One more thing before we move on to the next chapter. This book is about mindfulness and meditation; what those are, what they aren't and how to master both. In the Appendix, I discuss outside resources like apps, books, and podcasts. I am a big believer in all of these tools and there are some excellent meditation apps described in that chapter that can reinforce everything you learn in this book, so I want you to go ahead and pick one of the apps from the Appendix and download it now. I want you to start meditating *right away* and have every opportunity to succeed. So please, go right now and choose one of the recommended apps. They're all very good. Jump right in with some terrific, real time assistance.

CHAPTER 2

THE LANGUAGE OF MINDFULNESS

The premise of this book is that learning mindfulness is comparable to learning a new language, and it's true. Just as acquiring new linguistic skills can give you a fresh perspective on the world, adopting the principles and practices of mindfulness can, over time, do something even more profound. It can fundamentally change your relationship with the contents of your mind: your thoughts, moods and emotions.

Most people come to this practice with far more modest expectations. To put it simply, they seek a reduction in stress and an increase in calm. Typically, they complain of an excessively busy and racing mind; what they crave is peace on demand. This is a perfectly good reason to begin meditating but *striving* for these mental states is not what we are aiming for. Think about it – you can't clutch for calm or yank peace into place.

Using a variety of time-tested methods, you can train your attention to be where you want it to be, and if we want to calm ourselves down, that attention should focus on the here and now. As we intentionally bring our awareness to the present moment, a calmer state is a welcome *by-product* of our practice. By exploring your previously-ignored inner world, your very sense of self begins to shift. Indeed, by becoming still, you create the space to go deeper into the mystery of the human condition. This stillness, coupled with curiosity about your own mind, inevitably makes you quieter, and the quieter you become, the lower your stress levels.

Now I know this all may sound a bit too New Age-y, and I promise there'll be very little of that in these pages. But what the heck, while I'm at it, I'll add this: I believe that mindfulness can redefine your relationship to – and your awareness of – consciousness itself. Ponder that!

Trial and Error

To be perfectly honest, I tried to meditate any number of times in my life, going all the way back to the long-haired 1970s, but I never had any real training, so I was winging it. Typically, I would sit on my couch, close my eyes and do the worst thing a beginner can do: try to banish, suppress and rid myself of all thoughts. When I found this to be utterly impossible – because it is – I would deem myself the world's worst meditator, quit and maybe try again the next year, but always with the same results.

Through this book, my aim is to help you avoid all the mistakes I made by blowing up all the usual and unhelpful misrepresentations that still make the rounds about meditation and replacing them with practical, learnable and accurate instruction.

Unlike learning French, Greek or Chinese, Mindfulness is a language that's very simple and, at the same time, deeply challenging. It's simple because it can be boiled down to just sitting, closing one's eyes and paying close attention to the rhythms of your breath. Want to stop and try that now for 30 seconds?

EXERCISE:

Set a timer for 30 seconds.

Close your eyes.

Pay close attention to the rhythms of your breath for the entire 30 seconds.

No doubt you saw how difficult this simple task really is. Perhaps you were surprised to see that your mind wandered almost immediately before you remembered to come back to your breath. Not to worry, that is perfectly normal! You are doing fine. We will address the phenomenon of your wandering mind soon enough.

Once-and-Future Practice

I call it the Once-and-Future practice because it draws on an approach that's as ancient as contemplation itself, and as current as the "secret sauce" used by top performers, athletes and CEOs to gain an edge over the competition. The good news is that you can learn to be fluent in the fundamentals of Mindfulness within the pages of this book.

The not-so-good news is that, just as in learning any new language, you will absolutely need to practice in order to become proficient. And this practice takes a very specific form. Yes, you'll have to meditate. I know for some of you that'll be a deal breaker and it may be quite hard at first, but trust me, eventually you'll look forward to it and wonder why it took you so long to create this magnificent new habit.

After nearly seven years of daily meditation practice, I can attest to how this practice can fundamentally change both your inner and outer life. For me, it's not only improved my concentration and mental clarity, it's enhanced my capacity to provide myself, and others, with more kindness, acceptance and compassion.

While becoming fluent in the language of Mindfulness, I am still speaking my native language of English, but all manner of words now carry more meaning for me; words like awareness, consciousness, gratitude and compassion now inform how I am in the world.

The Many Meanings of Meditation

To some, it may seem ironic to discuss meditation in the context of learning a second language. After all, the most common perception of meditation is that it's primarily a non-verbal pursuit. Meditation, we're often told, is a path of silence and stillness; a way to enhance our understanding of our thoughts, feelings, moods and physical sensations. So, it may seem incongruous that the entrance to the world of wordlessness would be words, and yet, as human beings, words are all we have to effectively communicate.

In the modern world, the word meditation itself is used loosely and sometimes inaccurately. People use the verb "to meditate" when they mean thinking or planning. To meditate on a particular question or topic is to get involved in a preponderance of thinking about it. "Let me meditate on the matter and get back to you."

Others use it to refer to daydreaming or even fantasizing. For the most part, when I use the word meditation in this book, it will refer to what we call a "formal" practice, a defined series of established techniques that involve sitting still and using concentration to calm the mind. While I may use the term "formal" when I refer to our sitting practice, I don't want that to scare you. We are not required to sit cross-legged on the floor or engage in ancient rituals. Formal simply means to sit quietly with dignity and purpose, using both your intention and attention to create the optimal conditions for meditation.

This formal practice of mindfulness and meditation originated with what in Buddhism is called Vipassana Meditation. Vipassana is a word from the ancient Pali language that scholars believe the historical Buddha spoke, which translates to "seeing things as they really are" or "a clear awareness of exactly what is happening as it happens."

Another important Pali word is Samatha, which can be translated as "concentration" or "tranquility." Samatha is a state in which the mind is brought to rest, focused only on one item and not allowed to wander. Together they are the foundation of an ancient system of training your mind, a set of exercises dedicated to becoming more and more aware of your own life experiences.

Personally, when I was in my hour of need, if someone had said to me, "Nick, you're a hot mess, you should really try some Vipassana meditation," I would have run right out the back door! But the words I heard, and read, were words like *secular, logic, common sense* and *neuroscience*, and so I felt secure enough to try it.

Jon Kabat-Zinn and the Evolution of Mindfulness

While there are many ways to describe the big ideas behind mindfulness, millions of Americans were first introduced to them on prime-time television on December 14th, 2014. That's the night that Anderson Cooper ran a story about mindfulness on CBS's *60 Minutes*. Anderson's voice-over told the story of an MIT-trained molecular biologist named Jon Kabat-Zinn, a relative newcomer to American Buddhism. Jon was on a ten-day silent retreat when he had an epiphany.

While his own meditation practice was invaluable to him, he conjectured that its setting within Buddhism would prove a barrier to most people. He wanted to demystify, Westernize and modernize this wise and ancient practice; a teaching that was developed in India over 2600 years ago.

His vision was clear: to create a secular, i.e. non-religious, form of mindfulness so that many more people, from all walks of life, could have access to it. Kabat-Zinn understood that the innate human capacity for mindfulness was too valuable to belong to any single religion or tradition, so he created a curriculum to teach it without any shred of theology. He called it Mindfulness Based Stress Reduction (MBSR).

Today, mindful meditation is being taught and practiced in public schools, hospitals and police departments. Businesses have adopted it, first in Silicon Valley and now in all manner of legacy companies, including the Ford Motor Company Headquarters in Dearborn, Michigan, where I personally taught mindfulness.

It's also gaining traction in the military, in pro sports locker rooms, and even on Capitol Hill, where Congressman Tim Ryan of Ohio leads mindfulness sessions for congressional staffers seeking some bipartisan peace amidst the political chaos.

Having read these examples you might already surmise that there's no sitting cross-legged, no orange robes, no incense, no chanting or pan flutes required. What is required is curiosity about how your mind actually works. This is the level of curiosity about your mind, thoughts, emotions, reactions and relationships that you will bring to your practice.

While it may not be Buddhism, it is a meditation that uses concentration techniques focused on the physical (body sensations, breathing and sensory awareness), as well as every kind of mental event (thoughts, moods and emotions).

At the risk of sounding wildly obvious, let me stop and say this: it's not enough to just learn about the ideas and theories around this practice; one must actually meditate – almost every day – to benefit from meditation. When we do, we tune in to our body, we observe the nature of our feelings, and start to change our fundamental relationship to our thoughts, all in a spirit of curiosity and non-judgment, two foundational qualities we want to bring to our practice.

CHAPTER 3
DEFINING MINDFULNESS

When you decide to tackle a new language, one of the first things you'll learn is how to identify yourself. In French that could be, "Je suis une femme" or "Je suis un homme," which translates to "I am a woman" or "I'm a man." Beyond gender, you'll want to be ready when someone asks that threshold question, "Who are you?" Your answer may veer toward your profession (I'm a writer), or your religion (I am Catholic), or your relationship to someone (I'm Nick's niece).

Within a mindfulness practice, you'll soon discover that the question, "Who are you?" is something you'll be asking yourself – A LOT - as in, "Who am I, really?" In the same vein, even saying the words, "I am," carries fresh significance when you enter a new world of self-inquiry.

These simple words will inexorably lead you closer and closer to your core identity; the *you* that's beyond persona, roles and beliefs. Mindfulness helps you look directly at what

– and who – you really are. Once you are comfortable in a contemplative setting, you'll be able to say "Je suis mindful," with confidence. But let's not get ahead of ourselves; let's begin with the basics.

Mindfulness is Being Present

Mindfulness. It's a pretty straightforward word. In a general sense it means to pay attention, but in the context of this book it's more than that. Mindfulness means paying attention to what is happening right now, both in and around you. When you're being mindful, you're more aware of what you're thinking, feeling and doing, as well as who you're with and the circumstances you're in.

It's remarkable, really, once you get into it. You sit and know you're sitting, eat and know you're eating and, most importantly, think and know you're thinking. There is so much to be aware of. This might seem trivial, except for the inconvenient truth that we: (a) are rarely attentive to the present moment; and (b) are disposed to deviate, repeatedly, from the matter at hand.

Think about it: one minute you're fully engaged in a task, perhaps an important conversation or endeavor. In the next minute your mind takes flight. In the blink of an eye you've lost touch with your immediate environment and are engaging random thoughts that usually land you in the past or the future. There's a reason this is called being *absentminded*.

This situation is far from optimal for obvious reasons. Right here and right now is all we really have. The past – whether five minutes or five years ago – is gone, never to return. The future, be it ten seconds or ten years ahead, is pure fantasy and speculation. This moment, *right now*, is the only moment that exists, period. Full stop. As you read this sentence, this is your life.

Imagine, after all these years, finally waking up to the reality that these fleeting and instantaneous cognitive sparks *are* your actual life. Put another way, what we train our attention on is our reality, one moment at a time. It's not your name, your career, your relationships or even your memories. It's only now, and now, and now; and the more you're absent from all these *nows*, the closer you are to a kind of sleepwalking through life.

The good news is that there is a method of attention training that's at once ancient and cutting edge, and it's called mindfulness. Once you teach yourself this new language, no matter how often, or how far, you drift away, your fluency in Mindfulness will pay off by allowing you to snap back to what matters: where you are, who you're with, what you're doing and how you're feeling, in this new moment.

Mindfulness Rising

The fact that you are reading this book is a testament to your commitment to achieving some level of fluency in Mindfulness. Its popularity in the western world has skyrocketed in recent years. It's on the cover of magazines and in the evening news. Celebrities swear by it, scientists study it, NFL quarterbacks practice it and business leaders offer it to their employees to impede burnout.

These endorsements were important to me when I began studying mindfulness, as I too was stuck with an outdated impression of meditation. I thought it was too religious, too spiritual and too self-indulgent. I might even have joked that the practice was a form of navel gazing. Thank goodness I was disabused of these unwarranted impressions and I hope I can do the same for you.

There are many ways to describe mindfulness, but for my money, here's the definition that is as concise as one can make it: *Mindfulness is paying attention to the present moment non-judgmentally.* These nine words carry enormous potential for those who want to study their significance.

Here are five characterizations – all written by mindfulness experts – that point toward the same phenomenon:

1. Mindfulness is simply being aware of what is happening right now without wishing it were different; enjoying the pleasant without holding on when it changes (which it will); being with the unpleasant without fearing it will always be this way (which it won't).
- James Baraz, Berkeley-based Mindfulness Teacher

2. Mindfulness is the aware, balanced acceptance of the present experience. It isn't more complicated than that. It is opening to or receiving the present moment, pleasant or unpleasant, just as it is, without either clinging to it or rejecting it.

- Sylvia Boorstein, psychologist and leading teacher of Insight Meditation

3. Mindfulness has many synonyms. You could call it awareness, attention, focus, presence or vigilance. The opposite, then, is not just mindlessness, but also distractedness, inattention, and lack of engagement.

- Lifehacker.com, a blog about life hacks and software

4. Mindfulness isn't difficult. We just need to remember to do it.

- Sharon Salzberg, meditation teacher and NY Times bestselling author

All of these quotes can help us understand what mindfulness is, but it's the third one, the *Lifehacker* quote, that helps us see what it is not. This description helps us appreciate that the flip side of mindfulness can be a real problem.

It's important to recognize that the words *distractedness, inattention* and *lack of engagement* are a painfully accurate portrayal of how most of us spend many of our waking hours. Here then are some examples of mind*less*ness that you may be able to relate to:

1. Have you ever driven your car and arrived at your destination only to realize you remember almost nothing of your journey?

2. Have you opened a bag of potato chips and then wondered why, suddenly, you're holding an empty bag?

3. When you take a shower in the morning ask yourself this; are you experiencing that nice hot shower or are you busy reviewing what you're going do, say, meet or email later that day?

4. When your loved one asks you a question or shares a story about their day, are you really listening or are you too busy with your phone?

If any or all of these situations sound familiar to you, you are not alone.

The Pitfalls of Autopilot

When you're not mindful, you're on autopilot: a cognitive state in which you act with little or no self-awareness. In this condition we are reflexive, reactive, unmoored, adrift, neither here nor there. It's no wonder people often complain of feeling lost in their lives.

There's an old expression that says, "A wandering mind is an unhappy mind," but this is also the title of a 2010 study that determined that most of us are truly "checked-out" a good portion of the time.

Harvard University researchers Daniel Gilbert and Matthew Killingsworth found that most people are thinking about what is *not* happening right in front of them, almost as often as they are thinking about what *is* happening. Their conclusion was that living on autopilot could leave us unstable and vulnerable to anxiety, stress, depression and reactivity. The bottom line is that the more our minds wander, the less happy we tend to be. In the chapters ahead we'll address ways to mitigate this all-too-human trait.

The good news is, there are specific meditations that are very helpful for one's equanimity, i.e.: one's mental calmness, composure, and evenness of temper, especially in a difficult situation.

Right Now, it's Like This

Right Now, It's Like This is an invitation to explore what is truly present. It works by repeating the words silently to yourself in meditation. It's an invitation to accept, not push away, whatever is weighing on your mind.

This is one of the keys to becoming fluent in Mindfulness: stopping just long enough to identify what's happening in your head; seeing your thoughts as *just more thoughts,* and trying not to get too carried away by any one of them. It's our real-time reactivity to these unexamined thoughts that gets us in real trouble, especially the ones that trigger emotions, which is most of them.

But if you gain a modicum of objectivity about them, you can choose how best to respond to their promptings. As you may have guessed, this isn't easy. As we've seen, the human mind often feels like a wild horse (or a multitude of wild horses) running recklessly in all directions. On top of that, like any animal, it's always scanning for threats, which for us is almost anything that takes us out of our very narrow comfort zone.

Right Now, It's Like This. Repeating this phrase quietly to yourself is intriguing; a kind of mantra that lets you see that each time you say, *It's* there is a whole new *this.* Say it again and there's a new new *this.*

These five meditative watchwords also help you connect with direct experience, the more immediate and tactile way to explore how things are right now.

Regardless of what emotion you're feeling; whether joy or grief, anger or calm, happiness or sadness; the *Right Now, it's Like This* phrase whispers that (a) it's okay to feel it, and (b) it won't last; it'll pass. Everything does. Let's give it a try...

EXERCISE: RIGHT NOW, IT'S LIKE THIS...

1. Find a comfortable place to sit at a time when you won't be disturbed or distracted. A chair, couch or cushion on the floor, wherever you are most at ease. Set a timer for three minutes.

2. Sit in a posture that is relaxed and yet dignified, one that lends itself to being awake and alert.

3. Settle into your body, your sense of being. Feel your body in the space of the room; now feel gravity holding you gently in that place.

4. Allow your eyes to close; this can better help you enter the internal world.

5. Start with a few deep breaths, allowing them to wash over you. This helps the breath to find its natural rhythm effortlessly. The tone is relaxed and aware.

6. When you're ready, gently and silently say these words to yourself: "Right now, it's like this." Say it again. And again.

7. Say it in union with your breath. Emphasize a different word each time you say it, to keep it fresh. Sometimes the word "now" is prominent, or "this."

8. As you do this, feel what these words mean, because the meaning will change every time you say it. It changes because ten seconds ago – and ten seconds from now – are completely different moments. Each has a different NOW, and a brand-new THIS.

A word of warning: even though you are focusing your attention on this phrase (in conjunction with the breath), your mind *will* wander, 100% guaranteed, as thoughts, memories, and plans arise and pass away.

No problem! This is natural. The moment you realize you've gone down a rabbit hole, you're already back – to this moment, this breath, this…THIS!

This is a moment of wakefulness.
This is the practice.
You got this.

CHAPTER 4
DEFINING MEDITATION

Defining meditation is a tall order. First of all, it's a wildly loaded word, burdened with all manner of unrealistic expectations and exotic connotations that make people feel it's either out of reach or not relevant to their lives.

I can assure you that neither of these things is true, but when I was first exposed to meditation, I too was full of skepticism. Granted, I was just 16 years old, it wasn't mindful meditation, and I had the attention span of a fruit fly! Here's the story.

Transcendental Meditation

It was 1968 and my mother had become interested in Transcendental Meditation, better known as TM. In her wisdom, she thought I might find it interesting too, and I was quite curious, but for all the wrong reasons. That was the year the Beatles were hanging out with their guru, Maharishi Mahesh Yogi in India and honestly, as a rabid Beatles fan, that was good enough for me!

I went to a free lecture and later, when I arrived for my first lesson at the TM center in Washington, D.C., I was the youngest attendee there. Like everyone else, after instructions were given, I was provided a secret Sanskrit word as my mantra. The impression I got was this: my pathway to peace would be found via my total focus on this ancient word. My TM mantra was not to be said aloud, written down or even deliberately thought of outside of TM practice. Practice was a strict protocol, twenty minutes twice a day, morning and night, no excuses.

I was quite apprehensive at this point, but decided to give it a try. For three days I repeated my mantra over and over again and here were the results: I got bored, restless, distracted and impatient. I gave it up quickly (as did my mother a few months later) and for many decades allowed this failed attempt at TM to color my attitude toward the whole subject of meditation.

In fairness, TM is very effective for millions of people around the world, but for me it was simply too soon, too foreign, too associated with a single, charismatic teacher... and too expensive, as it costs real money to get your mantra.

Fast-forward 44 years and, as you read in Chapter One, My Rough Road to Mindfulness, when I was introduced to mindfulness and meditation after the hellish end of *Border*

Wars, this time I was ready. I was motivated and, thank goodness, there was no guru, mantra or fee!

The bottom line is this: mindfulness and meditation are within everyone's reach and with virtually no barriers to begin. That's one reason people in every walk of life have made it part of their lives. Today meditation is as accessible as an app and as American as apple pie, but what is it exactly?

The image of the sitting Buddha appeals to us because his expression is so serene. When I'd see one, long before I meditated, I'd think, "That's what I want: calm, balance, introspection; maybe even enlightenment." Those same images may have attracted you to pick up this book and that's great, but here comes the hard work of making meditation look so effortless.

Meditation: The Easy Explanation

In the last chapter we touched upon what it means to be mindful; to become more aware and receptive to the present moments of your life. The number one way of achieving that end is to practice sitting meditation. If fitness is your goal, then going to the gym is how you'd get there. If mindfulness is what you want, then meditation is the way. Here's a quick explanation of how to meditate in the simplest possible way. We have a much more detailed version of this same exercise in the next chapter, but this will give you the basic feel for it.

EXERCISE: BASIC STARTER MEDITATION

1. Set a timer for however long you want to meditate; start with five minutes. You'll be able to go longer later, but five minutes is a good starting point.

2. Sit with a posture of comfort and some dignity.

3. Close your eyes. Make no effort to control the breath; breathe naturally.

4. Focus your attention on your body in the present moment; sit and know you are sitting.

5. Once settled, gently shift your attention to the breath. Feel each inhalation and exhalation fully. Breathe and know you're breathing.

6. When your mind wanders – which it will over and over again – notice your thoughts. Try to release them, and all judgments about them, and return your focus back to the here and now via your body and breath.

7. Repeat until your timer rings.

Judging from this description you might think meditation is rather easy and, at its core, you'd be right. What the basic meditation instructions above don't tell you is this: by training your attention in this manner, you quickly become the *observer;* the witness to the inner workings of your mind.

How is that? By willfully trying to stay focused on the body/breath, you immediately see the awesome power of the mind to disobey you. It's humbling but fascinating.

The key is patience and observation as we build our practice, session by session, employing something called *effortless effort*. It's that sweet spot between determined concentration and a peaceful letting go. And yes, while work is required to build a consistent practice, we don't want to be grasping for specific results. As the saying goes, over-expectation leads to an appointment with disappointment.

Scientist in a Lab

My hope is that you'll approach this practice with the drive and attitude of a scientist. Your mind and body are the laboratory and *you* are the experiment. By assuming this role you'll soon begin to gain some much-needed objectivity over your thoughts and feelings, and your patterns of thoughts and feelings.

And here's my favorite part: when you truly stop to look into your *own* condition, you're really looking directly into the *human* condition. In this way you can stop blaming yourself for your uncontrollable runaway thinking. We're all in this complicated, beautiful and messy situation together. This is one of the key benefits of sitting in meditation; it creates the best circumstances to allow you to step back and be increasingly impartial about what's really going on in your head. As a scientist, can you think of a more worthy experiment?

In this grand experiment, you'll soon be watching your thoughts appear out of nowhere, take you for a ride, decay and then disappear into the ether, only to be followed by another and another and another with only the most tenuous connection to each other.

Now you'll see them for the ephemeral phenomena they are: rapid, fleeting, redundant and often totally irrelevant to your present circumstances. In other words, not that helpful much of the time. Again, this is *not* your fault. It's just your turn.

We need to see this because we get in trouble when we chase, follow or act on practically every thought we have. This is called thinking with zero *awareness* that we are thinking. This is the goldfish that doesn't know it's in a bowl, or even in water. This is the trance of autopilot. To me it's like driving a car without a steering wheel or brakes or a map. When we're lost in our thoughts with no clue that we're lost, we are sleepwalking through our lives.

If it's true that your reality is what you pay attention to (and it is), then by sitting still and focusing on an anchor point, you are bringing yourself back to *the* most important moment in your life...this one. As you learn to do this, you'll start to loosen your grip on those thoughts that are coming at you at the pace of 70,000 a day.

Star of Our Own Movie

Of all the animals on earth, the exclusive and unrivaled feature of humans is our awareness of our own subjective experience; our realization that we are, in fact, conscious. We know that we are all living a unique reality. We even know that ours will end with our death. In a way we're starring in our own 3D movie that's unspooling frame by frame, and those frames are the micro-decisions we make every waking moment. These mostly unconscious choices are guiding the movie through the various locations and characters that make up our lives.

As we are the lead character, the whole film is from our POV (point of view). Like some early video game, there is no other camera angle. What we see, hear, touch, taste and smell is what we get, and so it's literally in our nature to quickly size things up. We inherited that skill from our most ancient ancestors some six million years ago.

To survive back then, the post-ape hominids had to hastily determine what was good vs. bad, edible vs. poisonous, safe vs. dangerous, friend vs. foe. Today this neuro-legacy translates into our endless (and often trivial) opinions, beliefs and judgments about ourselves, about others and the world at large.

As the eons passed, we developed into highly conscious mammals with an overly developed supercomputer in our heads: the prefrontal cortex.

The prefrontal cortex (PFC) is the region behind our forehead that's responsible for personality expression, logical thinking, control of emotions, planning for complex actions, decision-making and moderating social behavior. This newest part of our brain made us into *meaning-making machines*.

With our overactive PFC, we can't help but to instantly make up a story to fit all that we encounter. We see faces in clouds, understand the mood of others by their body language, and tell ourselves whole stories derived from a small sound in the other room. Moreover, in conjunction with the deeper-seated amygdala (the brain's fire alarm system; the trigger for fight, flight or freeze), we are also magnificent threat detectors, perpetually scanning the environment for anything hazardous that might push us out of our comfort zones.

Many of these "threats" turn out to be false positives; actual delusions resulting in erroneous deductions. Have you ever mistaken a coiled hose for a snake? Have you interpreted an unreturned phone call as a sign of deep disrespect, a glance as a scowl, a gaze as a come-on?

How many times are you convinced you know exactly what's happening, only to be proven wrong within seconds, hours, days or sometimes years? The problem comes when we invest too much in these mostly made-up stories; they quickly solidify as facts in our minds which can easily misguide our decisions and behavior.

According to Buddhist teachings, in every waking moment we are unconsciously discerning reality from three key categories: pleasant, unpleasant or neutral. Walk down any city street and you'll see what I mean. You'll quickly notice yourself making snap judgments about everyone and everything you see.

If your automatic reaction is unpleasant, what pops into your mind is that he, she, they or it are too tall, short, ugly, underdressed, overdressed, well made, shoddily made, too few, too many, too colorful or too colorless! If what you observe hits your pleasant button, then you quickly decide that he, she, they or it are attractive, interesting and noteworthy. Finally, if what you see is of no concern to you at all, then he, she, they or it are ignorable; all but invisible. Bottom line: if jumping to conclusions were an Olympic sport, we'd all have gold medals!

If you're honest, you'll begin to see yourself thinking, "I like it, I don't like it, or I don't care about it." This uncovering of your hidden auto-reactions comes with the territory when you begin to meditate. As you sit quietly and turn within, you become aware of these pleasant, unpleasant or neutral patterns in reaction to your own thoughts, memories and moods.

By slowing down and observing the present moment this closely, you gain a whole new window into how the process takes place. There's no question that a strong meditation practice can help us see ourselves more clearly and objectively so that, over time, we may learn to be more suspect of spur-of-the-moment opinions. A wise mindfulness teacher once told me to continually ask myself, "What else might be true right now…".

Myths and Misconceptions

Just as we explored words that indicate the opposite of mindfulness, e.g. distracted, mindless, unfocused, let's now talk about all the things meditation is *not*. We'll start with the number one myth about the practice.

I submit that if you were to ask ten non-meditators what the purpose of the practice is, chances are that nine of them would say it's to empty your mind; to clear it of all thoughts. This is the ultimate in fake news! If anyone tries to convince you to attempt that, they're doing you no favors. I know, because I made that mistake myself many times. It turns out that most people entertain this perception, so let's discard that idea once and for all.

If you have a human brain, you will have a ceaseless stream of thoughts in both your waking and dream states. Trying to stop them is a futile task; it's like going to the ocean's edge to stop the waves from coming ashore. It's also been said that your mind secretes thoughts just as your mouth makes saliva or your pancreas secretes insulin. In other words, that is its function. Trying to stop your thoughts in meditation guarantees only two outcomes: self-criticism ("I am a lousy meditator"), and disappointment ("I might as well quit"). I will suggest this: if ever you succeed in stopping your thoughts completely, you may well be dead!

With that said, please don't go on the same fool's errand that I did years ago, trying to stop or suppress these transient mental manifestations. Instead, don't fight them, but rather observe and loosen your grip on them. With practice you can learn to see and reflect on your many judgments and expectations and thus stay more open to all possibilities.

Here are four standard misconceptions about meditation. Each one will help you to understand what it *is* by seeing what it is *not*.

Misconception # 1 – *Meditation is just a relaxation technique.* The problem here is the word 'just.' While relaxation is a desirable and common by-product of meditation, it is not its ultimate purpose. Meditation is less about chilling out than about waking up. It's about knowing yourself from the inside out. It's also a way to understanding of the immense power of the mind to take you away from right here and right now.

Misconception # 2 – *Meditation means going into a trance.* Nope. Secular meditation is not a form of self-hypnosis. You are not trying to negate or subjugate your mind. You are not trying to turn yourself into a houseplant. As I said before, you're not going into a trance so much as awaking from one; the trance of being on autopilot.

Misconception # 3 – *Meditation is running away from reality.* Wrong! Meditation is running *into* reality. Insight meditation, which is another name for the kind of meditation we're learning, is a practice done with the specific intention of facing reality; to fully experience life just as it is, and to cope with what you find. It is not an attempt to forget yourself or to cover up your troubles, in fact it takes real courage to go face to face with yourself.

Misconception # 4 – *A couple of weeks of meditation and all my problems will go away.* Sorry, meditation is not a quick cure-all. If you are serious about your practice, you'll likely see some discernable changes pretty quickly, but really profound effects are months and years in the making. Let me remind you again, we do not encourage striving for a particular state or outcome. It's all about being more open to the reality that is here now.

Meditation Can Be Done Anywhere, By Anyone

To be clear, the word *secular* in *secular meditation* is an adjective pointing to attitudes and activities that have no basis in religion. However, not being religious does not mean that secular meditation is not spiritual. That's a much longer conversation – and open to some debate – but, to my mind, spirituality has to do with peace through purpose; feeling yourself as part of a larger tapestry. It means developing core principles and values around the meaning of life and your connection to others. Using this definition, people with a tradition of believing in a God, as well as those without any religious mindset, can gain from meditation. It's a significant act of self-care.

The issue of whether mindfulness and meditation are religious came up when I taught inside the Los Angeles County Men's Jail back in 2017. In this outdated, unsafe and decaying prison, I had the designation of being a Junior Buddhist Chaplain; junior because I was new and Buddhist because this was the only way one could work with the inmates inside the jail. To do so one had to be some kind of chaplain. Did I teach Buddhism in this facility? Very rarely. What I taught the inmates is what I am teaching you now: secular mindfulness via meditation.

There is a great tradition of using these powerful tools inside jails and prisons to help mitigate the suffering. In fact, one of my greatest teachers, Fleet Maull – a former 14-year inmate himself – is a renowned pioneer in this work. He and his teams have gone into countless houses of incarceration for over 25 years, places that are normally unreceptive to this curriculum of human flourishing. Fleet also runs the Engaged Mindfulness Institute (EMI) in South Deerfield, Massachusetts, and this is where I studied with him for my certification.

One day in the LA Men's Jail, I was working in a high-security cellblock talking to some inmates through the bars. Each cell in this area housed four men in cramped quarters with one stainless steel toilet in plain sight. It was sad and sobering.

I began talking to a couple of the guys when another inmate heard us and ambled over. He was Latino, most likely a gang member as his body was heavily tattooed, and after listening to our conversation he said to me, "Dude, I don't need that meditation stuff cause, ya know man, I'm like very Catholic." He showed me a big bleeding cross on his forearm, among other rather menacing images. After hearing about his troubled and religious background in the Boyle Heights neighborhood of Los Angeles, I told him that a meditation practice could still be of great benefit to him and I asked him if he prayed. He said he used to and still did on occasion, but it was really hard now in his present circumstances.

I explained that what I was offering were simple techniques to get quiet, turn within and regulate one's attention. I told him that perhaps he could use meditation to gain some perspective on his thoughts and emotions. He listened for a while then looked at me and said, "Dude, do you think that might help me when I try to pray?" I couldn't have been more pleased with his insight and told him yes, you can absolutely use this practice to get in touch with whatever higher truth you pursue. I said that the quieter he got, the more he could listen to what he really wanted to ask God.

Long story short, he tried it. Three weeks later, when I returned, he was excited to see me and said that in spite of some ribbing from his "cellies," he'd been meditating for about fifteen minutes a day. He told me how much it helped him to stay calm, all the while putting him closer to his God. He said, "Ya know what I heard? That when you pray, you are talking to God but when you meditate, you are *listening* to him." "Dude, you got it!" I shouted and we high-fived through the bars. I could tell just by looking at him that he was a happier guy.

Just as I told this prisoner, there's only so much talking or reading one can do about meditation; it's all about doing it.

EXERCISE: A SIMPLE MEDITATION PRACTICE

1. Sit comfortably. Find a spot that gives you a stable, solid, comfortable seat. Set a timer for the length of time you want to meditate; I suggest starting with 5 minutes and working up from there.

2. Notice what your legs are doing. If on a cushion, cross your legs comfortably in front of you. If on a chair, rest the bottoms of your feet on the floor.

3. Straighten your upper body, but don't stiffen. Your spine has natural curvature. Let it be there.

4. Notice what your arms are doing. Situate your upper arms parallel to your upper body. Rest the palms of your hands on your legs or wherever it feels most natural.

5. Drop your chin a little and close your eyes or just let your gaze fall gently downward. You don't have to close your eyes; you can simply see without focusing. Me, I prefer to close my eyes.

6. Feel your breath. Bring your attention to the physical sensation of breathing: the air moving through your nose or mouth, or the rising and falling of your belly or your chest.

7. Notice when your mind wanders from your breath. Inevitably, your attention will leave the breath and wander to other places. Don't worry. There's no need to block or eliminate thinking. When you notice your mind wandering gently return your attention to the breath.

8. Be kind with your wandering mind. You may find your mind drifting constantly. That's normal. Instead of wrestling with your thoughts, practice observing them without reacting. Just sit and pay attention. As hard as it is to maintain, that's all there is. Come back to your breath over and over again, without judgment or expectation.

9. When the timer is goes off, gently open your eyes or lift your gaze. Take a moment to notice any sounds in the environment. Notice how your body feels right now. Observe your thoughts and emotions.

So there, you've done it. You've begun. Even with this first "formal" meditation you can see that it's quite simple, but far from easy. We'll get into all that soon enough, but for now, let's lay the groundwork of your new practice with a deep dive into all things...sitting.

CHAPTER 5

THE FIRST VERB OF MEDITATION: TO SIT

As English words go, the three-letter word *sit* is as basic as it gets, but even the most rudimentary definition of the word sounds convoluted. According to one dictionary, "To sit is to adopt or be in a position in which one's weight is supported by one's buttocks rather than one's feet and one's back is upright." While this definition is correct, when it comes to your new practice, it just scratches the surface of what sitting means to a meditator. In this chapter we'll explore why we sit, how we sit, where we sit, when we sit and what we sit on!

Sitting Meditation

Sitting still in meditation is essential to a committed practice. It supports our concentration as we train our attention to commit, again and again, to the present moment. This in turn allows us to observe our individual condition, which, as I've said, is synonymous with observing the human condition. This is a fundamental insight that comes with meditation because no matter how separate and unique each of us thinks we are, we share 100% of the same ancient brain and evolutionary traits with every other human, living or dead. This realization can lead us to more kindheartedness towards others and ourselves as we come to realize that this business of being a humanoid is, very often, a complicated and painful condition.

For those reasons alone it's worth exploring the intricacies of sitting meditation in some detail. After all, monks and yogis spent centuries trying different physical postures; just think of all the positions you'll do in a single beginning yoga class. They found that sitting in stillness, undisturbed and cross-legged is the pose that helped focus them the most. But however we sit in meditation, our goal is to be seated in such a way as to establish alertness, dignity and focused attention.

We've talked about the power of attention, now let's add the power of *intention*. Your discipline and willingness to carve out time to meditate every day – whether it's for five, ten, fifteen or twenty minutes – is critical to your success, and here's a tip: start by doing it five days in a row, even for a short time, and see how you quickly become invested in your progress. Once you've strung multiple days together, you'll appreciate that frequency tops duration every time!

Aim for consistency, knowing that if you miss a day it's all right, because tomorrow is a new opportunity to get back on track. With this approach you will weave the fruits of your meditation practice – being more mindful – into your life. This is how you'll feel its increasing benefits.

Formal Sitting Meditation

Meditation isn't only about the mind. How you position your body is significant as well, but that doesn't mean you have to be uncomfortable. Getting your posture right is key to staying relaxed and alert instead of tense, slumped or spaced out. As you'll see, it's quite difficult to focus on the present moment without getting restless so you need to give yourself every advantage. Chances are, when you start, meditation will feel awkward and uncomfortable and you'll feel self-conscious. That's all okay and normal. Finding the best meditation posture and seating arrangement for you can take a while.

While navigating through our routine life, we tend to think of our body, breath, and mind as separate things, if we think about them at all. While meditating, however, we seek to blend them into one. We sit and we pay attention to the breath (or an alternative point of focus) in hopes of quieting the mind and body, but it's harder than it looks.

When you see someone sitting in meditation they might appear to be calm, dignified and unperturbed, but don't be fooled. They are human just like you, and their mind is overflowing with way too much information; literally from a lifetime of collecting it.

If you could get a peek inside their mind, you'd discover they feel like a novice fire juggler surrounded by clowns in the middle of an itinerant three-ring circus. The only difference between them and a non-meditator at that moment is they *know* it.

When a more veteran meditator goes to sit, he or she already knows they'll be entering the circus zone and they're okay with it. To others they may appear serene, like a swan moving gracefully upon the water, but just below the surface there's a lot of very fast paddling going on, despite their strong intention to tame their racing and agitated mind.

The Nuts and Bolts of Sitting Meditation

When acquiring the skills for formal sitting meditation, your first priority will be to anchor yourself in your body by assuming an upright posture that allows you to stay awake and alert. Once settled, try to accept whatever's going on with you right now, be it good, bad, ugly or otherwise. It's what's happening, don't fight it. Meet yourself where you are.

Americans sit for an average of thirteen hours a day. We sit in our cars, on the couch, at the office and in restaurants. But mindful sitting is different from ordinary sitting in the same way that mindful breathing is different from ordinary breathing. When we utilize our breath in quiet meditation, we're using it to: (a) anchor us in the here and now; (b) increase our awareness of our internal mental mechanisms; and (c) be witness to the power of the wandering mind.

When the subject of meditation comes up, most people recall images of a Buddha-like figure sitting cross-legged and upright with a straight back, hands in lap, eyes closed and a subtle smile. And rightfully so. The upright spine promotes vigor and attentiveness, while crossed legs provide a solid, stable foundation for one's session. I won't go into all the various positions you can use, but no matter if you sit on a chair, a couch or a cushion, these six pointers are true for all options:

The **Eyes** – There are two schools of thought: (a) the eyes are gently closed, or (b) the eyes are open, but with the gaze low and soft, looking in a defocused way toward the ground, floor or rug a few feet in front of you.

The **Chin** is slightly tucked to keep your cervical spine aligned.

The **Spine** follows its natural curvature; upright, yet natural.

The **Sitting Bones** are centered and stable; not perched too far forward or spread too far back.

The **Arms** are parallel to the torso, hands falling naturally on the thighs, palms up or down.

The **Knees** are below the hips, with ankles loosely crossed.

For what it's worth, I am an eyes-closed kind of guy. I find it easier to get interested in the inner landscape when I can make the outer one disappear. When you do close your eyes, you'll notice right away how your other senses (particularly hearing) leap to the foreground.

The importance of *all* five senses becomes clearer. Sight (yes, even with eyelids closed), sound, smell, taste and touch are now demonstrably important to your interface with the world. Knowing this at a granular level is all part of the meditation experience.

Within the stillness of this posture you'll not only pay far more attention to your physical sensations, but you'll begin to perceive your opinions, thoughts, and moods as well, for these are the fluctuating components that make up your inner world. In this way, the sitting posture acts like a garden in which the actual workings of your mind-body rise up, like flowers (sometimes with their thorns) into your consciousness.

We practice formal meditation in large part to understand that for a significant portion of our waking hours our minds are merrily (or not so merrily) going about their habitual gyrations. Your mind and my mind and your best friend's mind and your mother's mind and the mailman's mind – they too would rather think about almost *anything* other than what's actually happening in *this* present moment and environment.

Typically, gnawing thoughts about our past or anxious thoughts about our future turn out to be infinitely more compelling, especially to the untrained mind. I gladly acknowledge that *none* of us can stay present all the time. All that's really asked for is that we take some intentional pauses during the day; mindful pauses that give us more clarity as to our thoughts, feelings and situations.

Chair Sitting

As for the sitting itself, and contrary to popular belief, most modern meditators today do *not* sit cross-legged on the floor. They use the same kind of apparatus we all do: a chair. In fact, in the majority of the classes I teach, be it with police officers, corporate executives or college students, most everyone sits in a chair.

That being said, I don't want you to be intimidated by the notion of trying to sit cross-legged, on the floor or otherwise, as there are some real benefits to this approach. I do it because as soon as I cross my legs, I am physically committing to this time to meditate. Like in sports, I'm putting my game face on. I also like that it helps establish a strong foundation for me, like the shape of a triangle or a mountain. Please note, while I sit cross-legged, I do not use just a cushion because frankly I need the back support. I tend, therefore, to use a wide piece of furniture (a nicely upholstered chair or couch) for my practice. In a pinch I can always sit on a cushion with my back to the wall.

However you sit, your posture is important to the meditation experience. While we call it a *formal* practice, that doesn't mean you'll be asked to have a ramrod-straight back as represented by images of Japanese Zen monks in a temple. Upright yet relaxed, alert while calm. Here are the chief things to remember.

SITTING 101

Sit comfortably. Your body should not experience discomfort during meditation. Wear loose, comfortable clothing that doesn't pinch or cut off circulation. When you're starting out it doesn't have to be complicated. Having your feet on the floor anchors you to the earth; using the back of the chair supports you. Sitting up straight with hands resting on your knees or in your lap stabilizes you. The goal is to be comfortable in your body while allowing your attention to be focused on your chosen object of concentration.

Sitting: How, When and Where

No matter *how* you sit, put some thought into selecting *when and where* you sit. It's important to identify a practical time and place to meditate, be it at home or at work. If your company offers a "quiet room," use it, and if they don't, advocate for one! This choice of where and when is all about minimizing obstacles to the formation of this healthy new habit, making your daily sit as easy to accomplish as possible. The number one practical consideration is this: create a space in your home that can be your consistent meditation area.

Many people create a kind of meditation "nest" in their house, with favorite books on mindfulness, maybe a couple of photos and some favorite objects or precious stones. Some have a special room in their house so as not to be disturbed by others, while for others it's just closing the door to their bedroom.

All of this privacy is great, if you can pull it off, but please note: I am not advocating that everything in your environment be ideal before you can meditate! You do not need perfect lighting, music, incense or even complete silence. You meditate to be with things as they are – both on the inside and the outside – as you will learn to incorporate and adjust to anything that is less than ideal. I once took a six-week class sitting on horrible plastic folding chairs in a bare room with linoleum floors and buzzing florescent lights! The teacher was unmoved by our circumstance. "Good for your practice," he would say.

I once heard that a veteran meditator could meditate inside Grand Central Station's famous main hall and still have a good session, so…I tried it! I found a nice spot on the floor with my back against the wall, got comfortable and meditated for about fifteen minutes in a location that more than 700,000 people pass through every day. That's the entire population of the state of Alaska or the City of San

Francisco! The sound was, as you'd expect, cacophonous and wide-ranging, but I used the sounds themselves as the object of my meditation. This is a very legitimate approach – using sound as a way to bring oneself into the present moment. More on why that is later.

What to Expect

When you're new to meditation, it's very important to approach your practice as the radical act of self-care that it is, as opposed to seeing it as a chore – just another thing to check off on your to-do list. Once you've "come to the cushion" and settled into your preferred sitting position, chances are – if you're like so many who've come before you – you'll close your eyes with the hope and expectation that you'll have immediate feelings of peace, tranquility and serenity. No? Not happening? Still waiting for that PTS (peace, tranquility and serenity)? Welcome to the club and congratulations on being a normal human!

It's ironic, but the very act of stopping, getting still and going within presents the perfect circumstances for the untrained mind to explode with thoughts. It turns out that the very conditions you're creating to get calm – sitting quietly and undistractedly – triggers your mental mechanisms to run amok. No iPhone or laptop or person to distract you; you are now alone with just yourself and yes, it can be uncomfortable at first.

Here's a favorite metaphor. Imagine your mind is like a toy snow globe and you've been shaking it all day long. As you sit in meditation, applying the techniques we've been considering, the little flakes will slowly fall through the liquid to the floor. The globe is now calm and clear (you can see the miniature castle!) until you shake it again. If this doesn't happen right away, or on every sit, please have patience, it will come.

Final Thoughts on Sitting

As I've said before, this practice is far from easy. Coming face to face with yourself is a humbling, and often frustrating, experience. Nevertheless, this endeavor at radical self-care thrives on the combination of repetition and a compassionate heart. My firm belief is this: no matter what happens to you on the cushion, there's no such thing as a bad meditation session. Let me repeat that: *there's no such thing as a bad meditation session!*

If your body is restless and your mind is racing, the good news is that you're *aware* that your body is restless and your mind is racing. This is a real step forward in your practice (though it may not feel like it) because this new level of awareness means that you are not on autopilot. You are now the goldfish who has become quite curious about water.

CHAPTER 6

THE KEY VERB & NOUN OF MINDFULNESS: PRACTICE

If you spend enough time around 57th Street and 7th Avenue in New York City, you may well be asked for directions to Carnegie Hall. The query could be a sincere question from a lost tourist, but chances are, when someone asks, "How do you get to Carnegie Hall?" they just want to hear you say, "Practice, practice, practice…!"

The truth behind this nugget of American wit is obvious. Only the most proficient artists play the Carnegie and the only way they achieve that proficiency is through the Three R's: repetition, rehearsal and reproduction. In short, the Three P's: practice, practice, practice!

The same is true when you try to learn a second language because if you want to speak it, you have to practice it – and if you want to speak it quickly, you have to speak it a LOT. Repetition is the key.

Going over the same phrases again and again stores the information in your brain and makes it easier to recall. That said, most instructors agree that if you can immerse yourself in that new language (for example, living with a Parisian family while taking all your college courses in French) you'll progress much faster. No matter the method, you must be patient when learning a new language because it takes time and effort (i.e.: practice) to become good at it.

Practice and Practice

Practice is one of those words that goes both ways; it can be used as a verb (to practice) and as a noun (to have a practice). As a verb it means to perform an activity regularly in order to improve at it. As a noun it means a *way* of doing something, as in, "He made a practice of being punctual" or the actual application or use of an idea, as in having a meditation practice.

My feeling is that once you've made meditating a near-daily habit, you've turned practice from a verb into a noun. At that point it becomes *your* practice; something that you own, sustain, and cherish. As you begin the work there's a quiet sense of satisfaction that comes from sitting five, six, seven or more days in a row. And while it may be a bit of an ego trip to pat yourself on the back, you do prove to yourself that you have more self-control and discipline than you thought you did.

Interestingly, when we refer to our own practice, we should probably use the plural form, as there are a number of practices within our practice. Another way to say it is this: there are any variety of techniques we can employ in service to our overall practice.

Techniques

The bottom line is this: the more you practice (verb) the more you'll *have* a practice (noun), but you can't practice without practicing *something*, and that *something* is your technique. Once you find a technique that works for your brain, body and circumstances, you'll be much better equipped to stick with it.

What follows is a menu of tried-and-true techniques that I believe should be explored as part of a solid meditation practice. These exercises are all very effective, and some may work for you better than others, so if one does not work for you, simply move on to the next.

Concentration

How do you combat the chaos of an overactive mind in order to quiet down and connect with your interior being? The best way is to employ one of a number of concentration techniques. We use concentration to focus attention directly on some object, be it an image, a sound, the breath, physical sensations, a word or a phrase. Continually returning your attention to this object develops your ability to remain calm, focused, and grounded.

Mindfulness (paying attention on purpose to the present moment, nonjudgmentally) and concentration are like two wings of a bird. Both must work in concert when it comes to formal meditation. Concentration is often called "singularity of the mind" and it consists of compelling the mind to remain on one fixed point. That steadfast use of an anchor allows you to see just how powerful the mind truly is. Say you want to follow the breath (for instance) and yet the mind stubbornly has its own agenda. When you see and feel this mental tension you immediately know that meditation is one of the few tools available to objectively see your thoughts, the endless chatter and stories, come and go and come again.

Mindfulness, on the other hand, is a delicate function leading to refined sensibilities. It's like two partners working in a complementary way on the same job. Mindfulness is the sensitive one. It notices things. Concentration provides the power. Concentration does the actual work of holding the attention steady on that chosen object, while mindfulness notices when the attention to the focal point has gone astray. If either of these partners is weak, one's meditation is compromised.

We'll go into much greater detail on the abstract noun, Concentration, in Chapter 11. For now, we're going to start with some basic concentration techniques.

Mindfulness of Breath

The classic anchor is the breath.

Breathing. It's the first thing you do when you're born and the last thing you do when you end your time on earth. On average, a person at rest takes about 16 breaths per minute. This means we breathe about 960 breaths an hour, 23,040 breaths a day, and 8,409,600 a year. If you live to be 80, that adds up to 673,228,800 breaths (when you include all the Leap Years).

The unadorned truth is that the totality of your earthly experience is sandwiched between these two monumental events: your first and last breaths. How ironic it is then that we take something we do almost 700 million times in our lives for granted as much as we do.

The very act of getting curious and reacquainted with this most automatic of physical functions has much to recommend it. It's free, it's portable and it's rather indispensable; in fact, it's critical to remaining alive. As you concentrate on the breath you can feel the joining of the mind to the body and the body to the mind. Slow down and experience every breath and appreciate being able to do it.

Secular meditation does not ask you to breathe in any strange or exotic way. After a couple of deep breaths to get settled, you can go on with your ordinary inhalations and exhalations. Make them easy and predictable, and preferably through your nose. This will begin to slow down your monkey mind; downshifting your entire nervous system. You can pay attention to the whole breath or you can focus on any part of the process. For instance, feel the air coming into your nostrils cool and exiting warm; feel the air moving past the back of your throat and down the windpipe; feel your diaphragm rise and fall.

As you attempt to closely follow the breath you quickly discover that your mind stubbornly sticks to its own agenda and wants to take flight. When that happens you won't even realize it for a while. When you do wake up to your wandering mind, be it after ten seconds or three minutes, remember that you're meditating and come back to your concentration on the immediacy of the breath.

When you start to feel that tension between a focused and a wandering mind, you appreciate that meditation is a tool to objectively see the power of your thoughts in action. It can be alarming to witness the endless chatter, spinning stories, and escapist fantasies that circle through your brain but don't suppress or turn away. This is the circus we came to see!

I often teach my students to count their breaths as well. This technique helps by giving you even more to focus on. Count an inhale and an exhale as one. Inhale, exhale, two. Inhale, exhale, three, and so on. This process is a potent training in concentration but it too is not easy.

Many notice that their minds have wandered away before they can even count to *three* but with time and patience their ability to focus improves and they can get much further along in the count before they surrender to the random thoughts that seem far more compelling.

In breath-awareness meditation, your posture contin-ues to play an important role. A relaxed, upright posture will allow the breath to flow freely while embodying the quality of wakefulness. Other seated positions (slumping, lying down, etc.) tend to reinforce unwanted qualities like sleepiness, inattention and agitation. Proper posture and breath contribute to relaxed awareness.

After a while you can start to expand your meditations to include paying close attention to other anchors. These can include all manner of bodily sensations as well as sounds, your five senses or simple words that take the form of an inquiry or affirmation; more on that soon.

Verbal Labeling Meditation

If you still find yourself distracted by a lot of mental chatter you can use a technique called *verbal labeling* as an aid to concentration. For example, on the in-breath say quietly to yourself "breathing in." On the outbreath say "breathing out." This makes you aware of what you're doing right now. There are other ways in which you can label your thoughts that may work even better. Whatever works for you is the right way. Just get started and see what benefits this practice brings.

Labeling Tips

- **Useful or Not Useful** – This plain distinction can cover virtually all thoughts. As they appear, try and label each thought as *useful* or *not useful*. If a thought is useful you might stay with it for a while. The thought itself can become the object of your attention and this is perfectly acceptible.

- **Types of Thoughts** – You can tag your thoughts with greater specificity by sorting them according to their utility. Thoughts can be labeled as *judgment, planning, fear*, or *remembering*, for example.
- **Physical Sensations** – Another choice is to label according to body awareness. As you feel sensations from a part or the whole of your body, simply label them as *warm, sore, itchy, or prickly*, etc. Recognize them and let them go.

Sound Meditation

Take a moment right now to pause and just listen. As you allow your mind to settle into hearing, you start to understand that sounds have a comparable nature to sensations in the body.

Like sensations, sound just is; you don't have to go seeking it and you certainly can't close your ears. All you can do is pay attention to it or not. Sounds, both near and far, appear and then disappear. When a sound disappears, it doesn't leave a trace. Each recognizable sound is happening in real time along with other more subtle sounds. Together they create a landscape of audio that is unique to that moment. Due to their real time qualities, sounds are a wonderful anchor to focus on.

Even the most annoying sounds, like horns honking outside, the loud humming of a refrigerator, the blaring of an alarm clock, or a plane flying low overhead can be experienced in a new way when we bring mindfulness to them. Think about it – the annoyance you feel does not come from the sounds themselves, it comes from your interpretation of those sounds as "unpleasant" or "bad."

Remember, the sounds themselves are *always neutral*. Let me go wider with this idea: *all* circumstances are *inherently neutral*. They are what they are. There's objective truth (scientific and empirical) and then there's *your* truth. Yes, if you're hurting, your pain is your pain, but your actual suffering originates exclusively in the mind.

With unpleasant sounds we can shift our relationship with them from aversion to curiosity, allowing the sounds to be just as they are. If you want to use them as the object of your meditation that's an excellent idea.

The sounds, singularly and combined with each other, are unique in the history of the universe. Turn your attention toward them and hear how they rise and fall in volume and in relation to each other. Watch them move from background to foreground and back again. Listen to them being exquisitely in the moment as they come and go. What I think you'll discover is that this lessens their negative impact. Let's look at the kind of sounds we all encounter every day.

Background Sounds

When you are meditating with eyes closed, among the first things you will notice is the emergence of background sounds: traffic noise, the hum of a ceiling fan, voices in the hallway. As you note each one, try to let go of the habit of identifying with them and judging them. There's no need to spin a story about the airplane overhead or sirens on the street; instead just dive in on the pure sensation of hearing. In this way, everything you hear is treated as equal; beyond good or bad, pleasant or unpleasant.

Abrupt sounds

Sudden, shocking sounds that interrupt us can also bring us back to awareness. Someone drops a broom and the *swack* snaps us back from our wandering mind. Someone sneezes and we're back in the now. The arising of a loud leaf blower outside our window can wake us up to the present moment just when we've been lulled into habitual thought patterns. It may be unwanted, but it can remind us to come back to the present moment and leave our judgments behind.

Melodic sounds

Sounds that form a melody tend to arouse emotions, which is what we love about music. When we sit quietly we will inevitably notice melodic sounds. A chorus of birds greets the dawn. A patter of rain taps the windowpane. You can even meditate to music itself, though I recommend instrumental music without lyrics. Classical music is my preference. Listening to the rise and fall of any of these sounds can arouse feelings that don't need to be named or clung to. I often use the image of a conductor waving a wand to cue the helicopter above, the car alarm outside or the kid practicing drums next door. To me, when meditating, it's all one big glorious symphony.

Kitchen Concert

Since I began my practice I have been on multiple residential retreats that last from five to seven days. The one thing they all have in common is a commitment to practice Noble Silence. This means there is no talking for almost all of the retreat. I know that may seem harsh, even bordering on impossible, but after the first couple of days it gets a lot easier and as time goes on, it's kind of a relief not to be having a conversation all the time.

What we do is meditate a lot, forty-five minutes at a time. The daily routine is easy to remember: sitting meditation, walking meditation, more sitting meditation, then more walking meditation, then a silent lunch, then more of the same (with some quiet yoga thrown in) followed by a silent dinner. Because these are Buddhist-style retreats they have what's called a *Dharma* talk from one of the retreat teachers at day's end. When that's done, we quietly go off to bed. The next morning, we are up at 5:00 a.m. to do it all over again.

On the second night of my first five-day silent retreat I was in the dining room after dinner and found myself fantasizing about what I would tell my wife and friends back home when they asked, "How was it?" And there you have it. This marvelous and powerful retreat had barely begun and my mind was already *in the future* preparing to *talk about the past*! Can you see how bloody hard it is to stay in the present moment? I decided right then and there to close my eyes and try again to focus my attention.

Sitting and breathing, I became acutely aware of the myriad sounds all around me: people scraping food off their plates, dishes clanging into bins, hand washers rinsing silverware, pots and pans being cleaned and put away, chairs being moved and people walking around the room. No one was talking but the place was alive with sound!

Suddenly, in my mind's eye, I saw a symphony conductor in black tails, signaling and calling forth each sound with his baton. It all became music to me then – a decidedly postmodern opus of the most sophisticated kind – but it sounded wonderful and very real. It was the sound of Now. It was the music of the Moment. And I realized I could join in! I opened my eyes and started tapping the bottom of my plastic cup on the table, adding a fresh percussive element that gave the piece more urgency. Indeed, the symphony now had a brand-new cadence. If I had my way, this improvised concert would reach a crescendo and then, as people finished their chores, the music would slowly fade away. And so it did.

To experience this type of meditation, read the exercise below. You can read through the script first then do the practice. This can be done in a seated position, standing, or even lying down. Choose a position in which you can be comfortable and alert. Set a timer for ten minutes for the practice.

EXERCISE: SOUND MEDITATION

1. Take the next few moments to find a posture that gives you a sense of comfort and wakefulness. As you do this, become aware of your body naturally breathing.

2. Gently shift your attention to focus on your ears. There's no effort in hearing what's present; the sound naturally comes right to you. Center your awareness on the fundamental aspect of hearing sounds. They rise, they exist and then they fall away, just like our thoughts. Note that you can't un-hear what you hear, and that the sound or combinations of sounds are unique to this moment and will never be heard again.

3. As you engage in sound meditation, you can't help but notice how the mind creates stories associated with the sounds you hear. For instance, you might hear pieces of a conversation down the hall and then try to figure out the story behind it. Or a siren will make you wonder what the first responders are responding to. It could even trigger a memory of having been in an ambulance or police car yourself. Notice how these stories instantly rush into your mind? Please note: there's nothing wrong about any of that, but when you're purposely meditating, you don't need to do anything. Sometimes a sound is just a sound.

Open Mind Meditation

The flip side to Concentration Meditation is called by many names: open mind meditation, open monitoring or choice-less awareness, even natural mindfulness.

While most meditations *do* focus on a particular object (sounds, the breath, body sensation), open mind meditation is an *objectless* meditation. In open mind meditation we don't concentrate on any one object; rather we accept *whatever* rises into our consciousness and try not to react to or change it. The old saying, "It is what it is" applies here.

Feelings, sensations, memories and thoughts may arise, but we don't cling to them or try to avoid them; we just let them be. Open minded meditation is full acceptance of whatever the present moment has to offer, without directing your attention to any one part of it.

This technique has also been called *blue sky meditation*. It's wide open. You may start to see your thoughts floating by like clouds in a blue sky, moving along with the next breeze or breath. If you are in a funky mood it's good to remember that the blue sky is always there above the storm clouds. In like manner you know that your fundamental human consciousness is always there no matter what the fleeting contents of your mind are.

In this kind of meditation there is no telling where your awareness may take you. Every open mind meditation is going to be different. Your awareness might shift to the sensations in your body; perhaps an itch on your cheek, a pain in your back, or the growling of a hungry stomach. At other times your mind may wander inward and reflect on passing thoughts such as "What am I going to eat for lunch?" or "I need to walk the dog tonight." Or perhaps your awareness will shift toward a sound, a smell, or a gust of wind against your skin. It's all good as long as you let it all pass through you.

CHAPTER 7

THE ADJECTIVES OF MINDFULNESS: INFORMAL & NON-JUDGMENTAL

In my mind the title of this book is perfect. It's part of a successful series of self-help books titled "...as a Second Language. The other great titles in the series (also worthy of your attention) are *Parenting, Grief, Happiness, Creativity,* and *Success.* When Valerie Alexander, the publisher and editor of the series, asked me to write *Mindfulness as a Second Language,* I told her I couldn't have come up with a better title if I'd tried. Learning about mindfulness is much like acquiring a new language, for three reasons.

First, it awakens you to a wonderful glossary of words; words like meditation, intention, attention, awareness and insight, along with concentration, cultivation and contemplation. Second, the adoption of this practice changes your outlook on life by broadening your horizons, the same way speaking a new language does. And finally, this valued information – like a second language – progressively assimilates into your daily life if you are willing to practice it. It makes the familiar in life new again.

Informal Meditation, a.k.a. Routine Mindfulness

When you're not sitting in formal meditation you can learn to engage in what's called *informal practice*. This is the practice of mindful awareness in daily life. You don't carve out a special time for it; you pay attention, on purpose, to your body, thoughts, and emotions in the environment you're in. In this way you're weaving mindful moments into your regular routines by bringing more awareness to your everyday activities.

One of the top suggestions I use when teaching is, "When you're having that first cup of coffee in the morning, make sure you are really *having* that cup of coffee. See, smell, feel, taste and appreciate it." Here are a few other ways to wake up to the actual moments of your actual life.

Micro-hits

We know we can't be mindful *all* the time but we can consciously muster bursts of present-moment awareness throughout the day. For instance, when you feel a little restless you can tune in to your body, first by focusing on how your feet feel inside your shoes. Then you might notice whether your jaw is tight or loose. After that you might stand up a little straighter and open your eyes a little wider and take in what's really going on in and around you. Suddenly you've popped out of the random thought machine and dropped back into your real-time life.

Micro-hits are little chunks of time, ranging from five seconds to five minutes, when you pause in your day to make informal meditation your sole focus. You can be walking down the street, waiting in line, taking a minute before a meal, or just becoming still whenever you have a few minutes to spare. Sometimes when I'm driving and find myself at a red light, I remember to stop and drop into the now. I turn down the radio, feel my hands on the steering wheel and look around. I notice people on the sidewalk. I roll down the window and feel fresh air on my face, marveling at the patchy sky. I hear the sound of the city and, for a moment, I've escaped the circus of my mind.

Also, try bringing more awareness to the boring day-to-day stuff you tend to do unconsciously. Pay more attention as you're brushing your teeth, taking a shower, eating breakfast or walking to work. Open to your senses as you zero in on the granular level of reality. Remember eating one raisin back in Chapter One? Did you ever stare at a leaf to examine its network of veins? Or look at the sky so long you actually watch seemingly still clouds move, or listen to a song with your eyes closed and hear it like you never heard it before?

You can even remind yourself when to be mindful; you can choose a cue to shift your brain into a mindful mode. Passing through a specific doorway in your workplace or house; seeing your reflection in the window when walking by a store, or booting up your computer – just pick a cue that will remind you to breathe deeply and take it all in.

On an interpersonal level being mindful can result in really hearing what your friend is telling you at lunch, what your co-worker is handing off to you at work, or what your teenager is saying about her social dramas at school. Not all of it may be of great interest to you, but everyone wants to he heard and seen, just as you do. This is known as Mindful Listening and it's one sure way to become a treasured person inside your collective circle.

Background Awareness

If you intentionally shift your focus from your distracted mind to what's happening right now, you can really feel the difference. It's like waking up from a trance. When you bring your mind home to the present moment you might find that routine activities are far more interesting than you had thought. Washing dishes can be a tiresome chore or a watery, sudsy dance. Your commute home can be a tedious schlep or a great chance to breathe and decompress.

For instance, when working with cops, I tell them to slow down when they're putting on their uniforms and strapping on their gear. This is a moment for them to remember why they chose this profession and to pay attention to each step of the process. The belt with its radio, batteries, gloves, cuffs, taser and gun. The badge with its heavy symbolic meaning. Donning their uniform slowly and mindfully can bring a seriousness of purpose to the beginning of their day, renewing their commitment to protect and to serve.

Here's a list of suggestions for you to practice micro-hits of mindfulness and background awareness, starting with waking up and going through the day until you return to bed.

A Mindful Day

- Wake up early with gratitude for being alive
- Do a quick mindful body scan while in bed
- Notice your first thoughts of the new day
- Brush your teeth with awareness
- Practice shower meditation
- Make your bed mindfully
- Taste your coffee or tea with awareness
- Practice morning meditation
- Read inspirational content
- Prepare and eat breakfast mindfully
- Be present with your family
- Practice mindful driving
- Arrive at work ready to be productive
- Straighten up your desk and get organized
- Take a deep breath and open your inbox, then mindfully check email
- Make note of how you react to emails
- As you work, focus on the task at hand and decrease distractions

- Be present with peers
- Create mindful meetings
- Stand, stretch, and move
- Take a break from digital devices and go outside
- Mindfully end your workday
- Create a dinner ritual
- Wash dishes mindfully
- Mindfully review your day
- Practice guided sleep meditation

D.O.G.S.

Sometimes we all need a little help to remind us to come back to the here and now. It is so common for meditation teachers to continually advise their students, "Stay in the present moment." This refrain is repeated so often that it's been rendered an almost meaningless cliché, so I decided to go in another direction. This is a mindfulness exercise that's memorable, specific and instructional; one that leaves little doubt as to what it really means to be mindful in your daily life.

I call it D.O.G.S., which is an acronym for:

- **D**rop into your body
- **O**pen yourself to your senses
- **G**o to the front of your mind
- **S**urvey your thoughts.

Let me unpack this for you.

It's 6:00 p.m. and you're grocery shopping. You've filled your cart with groceries and are now scanning the queues, trying to figure out which checkout line will be fastest – but when you finally choose what seems to be the fastest line, you feel an instant pang of regret! Within moments you're 100% convinced you're in the wrong line as your mind quickly makes a series of snap judgments.

You're annoyed with yourself, with the slow customers in front of you and now particularly with the overly talkative cashier helping a woman who doesn't seem to know how to use a debit card! When that disaster is done, how dare he then have such a long conversation with the shopper just ahead of you? Doesn't he know you have somewhere to be? Your breath quickens as a tiny spark of anxiety arises. You rapidly scan the environment again for a possible escape but it's too late; you ain't going nowhere. This, my friends, is the perfect moment to practice D.O.G.S.

As you stand there in line, instead of beating yourself up and scowling at your fellow shoppers or the grocery checker, you should **Drop into your body.** That means feel your feet on the floor, your body in space, the temperature in the room and gravity holding you down. Move a bit, stretch, sway and settle into your human form.

Now **Open yourself to your senses**. Start with your eyes and look around you. Notice that you are in a retail miracle; a cornucopia of colors and sounds; an edifice filled to bursting with food, sundries and people. Note the mother coping with her fussy two-year-old at the end of aisle seven.

Look at the untied Air Jordan sneakers on the feet of a teenager behind you. Listen to the churn of voices and sounds that surround you. You can even smell the aroma coming from the hot food bar where folks are filling up little boxes. It's all there, just waiting for you to pay attention. This is a great time to watch people and, as you do, try to notice how many instant judgments you are forming about them.

This is where it gets interesting. I want you to **Go to the front of your mind.** What the heck does that mean? Let me explain. *Go to the front of your mind* is an instruction to pay close attention to what's happening *on purpose*. When you consciously do that, you tighten your focus and concentration as you lean into the moment.

The science behind this suggestion is this: the front of your brain is where your prefrontal cortex (PFC) lives. As mentioned earlier, this where we have what's called our *executive function,* which is associated with complex behaviors including planning and decision making. Individuals with strongly developed PFCs are more able to control their impulses and delay gratification.

As you do these things, thoughts will still arise, and they too can become a point of focus in this suddenly mindful moment. So now the *S* in D.O.G.S. is **Survey your thoughts**. What are you focusing on? Why? How important is that, really?

There you have it: **D.O.G.S**. Try it and then watch *yourself* reuniting with *your self* in the here and now.

Here it is again:

- **D**rop into your body
- **O**pen yourself to your senses
- **G**o to the front of your mind
- **S**urvey your thoughts

Mindful Farmers' Market

Just a few days ago my wife and I went to our farmers' market to buy fresh items from local farmers. For us, the market is more than just a place to buy produce and flowers; it's a chance to be out with our neighbors. That day, it was bright, sunny and cold and the place was packed with happy sights, sounds, smells and colors. Here the people-watching was excellent as parents, kids, street musicians and vendors filled the cordoned-off street with kinetic energy.

I used this opportunity to practice D.O.G.S – Drop, Open, Go and Survey – and soaked in the hustle and bustle with a fresh appreciation for my fellow human beings. I could see the whole scene as a moving mosaic of life. I also zoomed in on individuals: a father dancing with his three-year-old son to the music of an itinerant guitarist; the smile on a Latina woman's face as she handed us a tamale wrapped in corn husks; the family with five kids ranging from toddler to teens whose harried parents tried not to lose them in the crowd.

As we shared our tamale, I took the opportunity to see my wife anew and noticed her silver hair beautifully backlit by the bright sunshine. Later I enjoyed a coffee at a crowded café while she continued shopping. In this smaller space I heard various conversations as I savored the wonderful mundanities of people's everyday concerns. Once I got my coffee, I sat outside to wait for my wife. As I did, I purposely focused on my nice hot cup of joe, made just the way I like it, with a splash of half-and-half and some sweetener stirred in with cinnamon and nutmeg on top.

My mindfulness had me meditating on this brewed coffee as I drank it slowly, savoring its goodness while the parade of humanity strolled by. Granted, I was in a pretty good mood to start with this morning, but I have gone to this same market in both foul weather and a foul mood. Those conditions do make it far harder to get out of one's head and into the interior and exterior phenomena of the moment.

When we are troubled we tend to get smaller – to contract rather than expand. Instead of observing and celebrating this display of peace and commerce, my head would hold endless looping conversations with itself trying to solve whatever problem du jour was making me so distracted.

In moments like this, mindfulness can become a true refuge. If your mind is bouncing between past regrets and anxiety about the future, try to notice the fact that in the present moment you are, actually, safe and fine. Right here and right now, if you're not under immediate attack,

99 times out of 100 you are okay. It's then you realize that the only antagonist is the enemy inside your mind!

It's much harder to be mindful when you feel rotten or distracted by a perceived downturn in your life, but that's precisely the best time to observe the father dancing with his son; to notice the Latina woman's smile; and to be amazed at the family of five kids and their tired parents. This form of refuge is available any time you're willing to tune in to it.

Beginner's Mind

Once again, like learning a language, you can't just decide to be fluent.

You can't snap your fingers and speak Spanish on demand. You have to learn and practice, and then practice and learn some more. Practicing daily (or near-daily) sitting meditation is how you grow the power of mindfulness that will enhance your moods, make you more resilient and bring you closer to the ones you love.

These deliberate bursts of awareness teach us how to leave behind our fixed ideas and opinions and see the world (and everyone in it) with far less judgment. This fresh and non-judgmental view is known as *beginner's mind.* A beginner's mind is an open mind, an unbiased mind, a welcoming mind, and a curious mind.

To engage in beginner's mind, imagine it's the first time you've seen this thing, this person, or this situation. Try it as you open the refrigerator, listen to your offspring's endless stories about grade school friends, or watch the sunset. For a moment have no preferences. There is no good and bad – just accept and allow and be.

As you drop your preconceived notions, you might finally see the person, place or thing for what it really is. For so many meditators, new and veteran, it's a whole new way of being in the world, and the benefits are obvious. You become more curious, less cynical; more patient, less judgmental; more considerate and less grouchy. All of these qualities are most laudable.

CHAPTER 8

THE MINDFUL LANGUAGE OF THE BODY

Among the first challenges we encounter when attempting to learn a new language is how to communicate about our physical bodies. It's an essential component of standard literacy for any child or adult, so most Second Language instructors use visual aids to instill the fundamentals. Pictures, graphics, photos and drawings help to clarify the vocabulary used to talk about body parts and bodily injuries, as well as various maladies and illnesses.

Checking in

When it comes to the language of Mindfulness, one cannot overstate the importance that awareness of our body plays in our practice. It's not an exaggeration to say it's our very foundation. Awareness of the body is the bedrock of this training, and for good reasons. Nonetheless, those reasons would *not* be apparent to a casual onlooker seeing people engaged in meditation. They might grasp that people are sitting quietly in an upright position with their eyes closed, but they'd have no real idea of what's going on.

While the observer might be genuinely interested, others can find the whole topic quite unnerving. You might hear pejoratives about the practice when the unaware use terms like "navel gazing," while assuming that the practitioner is spacing out or lost in a trance. The irony here is stunning as this profound act of self-care, this embrace of stillness to go within, takes real commitment and courage. In this modern age of endless doing and distractions, to go face-to-face with yourself is an act of personal courage. This is certainly not checking out – it's checking in. It's not spacing out but rather waking up!

The Music of Mind and Body

In daily life the connection between mind and body is an essential component of our human experience, yet we often pay little attention to the data flowing up to our brains from below unless, of course, it's unpleasant, painful or the symptom of an illness. Elite athletes and dancers know how critical this connection is, but so many of us lead sedentary lives and are not very aware of the messages our bodies are trying to communicate.

Many years ago I took a class in hand drumming. It was a fun and well-attended drum circle class offered free of charge by the drum maker, Remo. It was also a clever way of selling lots of hand drums to the public. Every week, there were about fifty people in class and each session featured a new instructor, most of whom were professional drummers.

One week an instructor brought in a special stethoscope and an amplifier. To our amazement, she used these tools to amplify her own heartbeat. We could all hear the boom, boom, boom of her heart as a loud and powerful proof of life. When she began drumming to the rhythm of her own heartbeat, we quickly joined in. It was a remarkable feedback loop; the body's natural rhythm now exploding into a joyous sound made by a room full of amazed would-be musicians! From that initial rhythm we improvised, working ourselves into a drumming frenzy.

In a far more subtle way, this is analogous to tuning in to our own body when meditating, but here we need to get quiet enough to "hear" our senses, our body's functions and the rhythm of our breath. There is music in our own physique if we take the time to listen. And if we pay attention, we will discover the myriad notes being played in our feet, legs, pelvis, torso, arms, hands, shoulders, neck, face and head.

Neck Up?

There's no doubt that we live in a world that venerates thinking above all else, but again, like that famous goldfish who has no idea she's swimming in water, we are so used to being lost in our precious thoughts that we don't even know we're lost. Most of us are taught to identify 100% with our endless cascade of beliefs, despite their transient and suspect nature.

I asked this before and I'll ask it again: have you ever given much thought to the fact that your thoughts are really just small stories you tell yourself, each story reminding you of another and then another?

Some part of us can witness how these narratives appear, exist, decay and disappear. Where did they come from and where do they go? You have it and then it's gone, pushed out by a new one. Have you ever been curious as to their origin, their purpose or their effect on your moods and bodies? Even the word itself – *mindfulness* – makes it sound like a *head trip*, a neck-up activity, but this is decidedly not the case.

While many of you have come to meditation seeking inner peace and stress reduction (which you can certainly find), there's still a lot more to discover.

The truth is, when we meditate we are training ourselves to pay attention not just to our thoughts, but also to the direct sensations emanating from our bodies, including our five corporal senses: sight, sound, touch, taste and smell. This level of attentiveness is what allows mindfulness to bring us out of our heads and into our whole being. In fact, the facility to be "mindful of the body" is fundamental to liberating the mind.

Guiding Back to the Body

When I guide my students in class, I always begin by getting them into their bodies. I say, "Settle into your seat, chair or cushion. Get symmetrical, get centered and feel the points of contact with your feet on the floor and your legs and back in the chair." Once that's happened, I remind them, "As we come into this moment of transition – out of our hectic day into this quiet act of self-care – the fact that you're here and on the cushion does not mean you're *really* here. Indeed, your mind may be anywhere *but* here. Your body, on the other hand is 100% here and 100% now and it's just waiting for your mind to join with it."

Every time I say this it reminds me of the old TV announcers who used to intone, whenever there had been an interruption in the schedule, "We now rejoin our regularly scheduled program, already in progress." Think about it: your body is the program that's always already in progress and your mind is the interruption. As I write this, it's still amazing to me how the human mind so wants to resist the present moment; how habituated it is to the promise of something newer and more dramatic than whatever is happening right now.

It's true whether the drama in your head is from long ago or impending. If it's old, notice how you're still replaying it in your head. If it's yet to be, watch as you rehearse over and over what you might do or say.

While your body is engaged in navigating real life in real time, part of you is aware of how you instantaneously interpret the world around you. Objects, movement, noise, shadow, light, temperature and texture; your senses are dealing with them automatically while your conscious thoughts are most likely lost in the past or worrying about the future.

It may well be that the *last* thing you're truly aware of is your body's interactions with the world, and that could have dire consequences. As a case in point, the number of pedestrian accidents with cars have skyrocketed as one or both of the people involved were using their cell phones while in motion. The lesson here (while a little hyperbolic) is that *mindlessness* can be fatal.

The Reunion

How do you reunite body and mind? How can you become embodied – in the literal sense of the word – when your mind is gallivanting all over the place? Here are two exercises, both called *scans*, that will get you and *you* back on the same page. You can do these scans quickly; at your desk at work or standing in the kitchen at home. You can also try them as part of a deeper, longer and more formal meditation. Either way they are both enormously beneficial.

The first is a *sense scan*. The practice is to cycle your attention through the five senses while meditating. In no particular order, you bring your full attention to your senses of **sight, sound**, **smell**, **taste**, and **touch.** I like to think that going through the five senses is like a pilot checking all the instruments in the cockpit as she prepares for takeoff. I check through mine every time I sit in meditation.

By stopping and checking in with these sensory portals, we appreciate anew that everything we experience, and ultimately know, must come through one or more of these on-ramps into our consciousness. It's just another way that our practice puts us back in touch with our human condition.

Read the instructions below, then put this book down, sit tall in your chair, get quiet and cycle through your senses. Take your time and be as present as possible.

EXERCISE: THE SENSE SCAN

1. Sit and close your eyes. Begin by bringing your attention to your body as a whole. Notice how your body is seated and check your posture. Feel the weight of your body on the chair or the floor.

2. Start with **Sight**. Take a few deep breaths as you open your eyes briefly to take in the visual environment before you and then close them again. Do your best to see what you see. Are there patterns behind your lids illuminated by the sun or the light in the room? If you can, turn toward the light source to see these patterns more easily. Just rest in this closed-eye view, take it in and breathe.

3. Now turn your attention to **Sound**. Don't reach for it; just let it come to you. Big sounds and small ones, near and far. The hum of the refrigerator or the traffic outside; let it all be a symphony. When a sound starts to create a "story" in your mind, try and let it go. Have the sound be just sound. Be as present with it as you can without judgment.

4. After a while, tune into your sense of **Taste**. Savor what lingers after that last cup of soup or coffee or cough drop. Feel the inside of your mouth with your tongue as a new experience.

5. Now switch to your sense of **Smell**. Imagine you have a dog's nose. Think of all the odors that a dog would sense in this same environment. Just rest in the odors that you can perceive.

6. Finally, engage your sense of **Touch**. This can entail your whole body or just your two hands resting on your legs. It's the feeling of your clothes, a breeze through the window or the temperature in the room.

7. Tune in and be aware of your body, feeling the weight and pressure, vibration and heat. Soften your jaw. Let your face and facial muscles relax and be soft. Now notice your whole body once again and imagine it as a cloud of sensations. Take one more breath and when you're ready, open your eyes.

The Body Scan

Like the sense scan, the body scan can be done as a brief check-in or as a full-blown investigation into sensing every part of the body. This type of scan is an important part of the secular mindfulness agenda and there are many excellent guided body scan meditations available in apps or online websites. At the end of the book you'll find a resource guide to my favorites.

As the name implies, the body scan meditation focuses attention on sensations in the entire body. The purpose of this practice is to cultivate the ability to notice what is being experienced in the body. This includes all of the body's systems: bones, skin, internal organs, digestion, and so on.

When you're feeling frazzled it's common to carry stress in your body in the form of tense shoulders, a stomach in knots, shallow breathing or teeth clenching. Often when people carry this kind of stress, they're not even aware of it. This scan is particularly useful in understanding how physical experience is tied to emotional experience. It's effective in relieving stress for two reasons. Yes, it settles the mind, as do other forms of meditation but it also deals with the physical components as well. In this way, the body scan works to help break the cycle of physical and psychological tension that can feed on itself in an endless loop.

Let's try this, but please note that you may experience unexpected emotions during this practice. Focusing on your body can stir up stored feelings. You may also become sleepy. Both of these states are fine and to be expected. The important part of the practice is to stay connected and aware of your experience without judgment. You can try this shortened and modified body scan meditation right now.

EXERCISE: THE BODY SCAN

1. Do this lying on your back on the floor. It's good to use a yoga mat if you have one. Begin by bringing your attention into your whole body. Close your eyes.

2. Feel the weight of your body on the floor and take a few deep breaths. Try to relax deeply. Notice the back of your heels in contact with the floor. Note the sensation of your feet touching the floor. Feel the weight and pressure, vibration, heat.

3. Notice your legs against the floor and any pressure, pulsing, heaviness, or lightness. Feel your back against the floor. Bring your attention to your stomach area. If your stomach is tense or tight, let it soften.

4. Take a breath. Sense your hands. Where are they? Are they tense or tight? Allow them to soften. Notice your arms. Do you feel any sensation in your arms?

5. Soften your shoulders. Notice your neck and throat. Let them be soft and relaxed. Soften your jaw. Let your face and facial muscles be soft.

6. Notice your whole-body presence. Take a breath. Be aware of your whole body, as best you can. Take another breath. When you're ready, open your eyes.

Both the Sense and Body Scans, like all the meditations you'll learn, are part of your overall practice. As you've no doubt gathered, we don't do these things in a one-and-done kind of way. We do them to continually sensitize ourselves to the reality of living a human life inside our human body.

As you've progressed through this book, you've had many chances to try various meditations. There are more in store. Some are concentration-based while others are used to cultivate qualities you'd like to enhance in yourself. Some will work for you and others won't. I encourage you to use these resources to create your own practice. This is no small thing to say; your practice is your practice and no one else's. It's something you'll continually build and re-build throughout your life. Congratulations on your progress so far. Let's keep it going!

CHAPTER 9
THE MINDFUL LANGUAGE OF FEELINGS

Second language teachers work to construct a robust emotional vocabulary early on with their students, teaching words like happy, sad, worried, excited, and scared. Having a viable emotive lexicon is a critical component of literacy, necessary for both children and adults to engage in social interactions and regulate their emotions. At the same time, many instructors like to make the lessons fun and memorable, adding some spice by giving students a chance to try out some choice four-letter words (which I won't repeat here) along with interesting curses, spells and jinxes.

Watching our Emotions

Insults and curses are designed to vent frustrations and strike back at the perceived causes of our emotional unrest; something we humans have in abundance. Our brains have been hard-wired to *feel* our way to survival; to feel scared, to feel love, and even to feel hatred. Since our early primate ancestors rose from all fours to walk upright, our smorgasbord of emotions has evolved to be our greatest survival advantage, helping us to pass along our genes to succeeding generations.

Today in a high-tech yet troubled world, our emotional life can use all the help it can get. While psychotherapy, antidepressants, a healthy diet and exercise are all important resources, I have found that there's a deeper well to tap for well-being and self-regulation. Without trying to sound hyperbolic, I believe your newfound meditation practice has the potential to fundamentally change your relationship to your mind; to alter your basic understanding of your thoughts, moods, attitudes and feelings. This, my friends, is a very big deal and worthy of your efforts.

In earlier chapters we talked about how a committed meditator takes on the role of the witness, the observer of his or her thoughts. This is the real secret of the practice – the ability to develop a newfound distance, thus gaining much needed perspective over our emotions and the thoughts that trigger them. It's been determined that we can, for instance, be truly angry for only a very short period of time. It's our mind that keeps stoking the flame with continuing righteous and defensive thoughts, each one a mental log we throw on the fire to keep the anger going.

EXERCISE: ONE-MINUTE NON-MEDITATION

As a reminder of this important idea, let's pause here briefly to check in with ourselves. Stop for just one minute and put the book down. Set a timer. Close your eyes and observe whatever's going on in your head and heart right here and right now. This is an exercise in pure observation; whatever thoughts, sensations or emotions arise, just see them and let them be, no stories or judgment necessary. Notice how fleeting each one is. How hard to hold a single emotion. When done, resume reading...

Picture yourself with the sustained meditation practice you were dreaming of when you bought this book. Imagine spending time on a regular basis quietly by yourself and with a single intention – to uncover what's going on in the inner sanctums of your mind, body and heart. What a radical idea: to become truly interested in your own mental machinery!

The truth is, the very act of meditating asks us to examine the most basic aspects of our inner lives. When you're committed to the investigation of how your mind decodes meaning from experience, that's when you can make the real changes toward greater happiness.

All it takes is a willingness to return again to your quieter, introspective self; a self where your *intention* guides your *attention*, returning increasingly to your actual unfolding life. As I have said before, this is nothing less than a radical act of self-care and one that will benefit both you and those around you.

What Have You Done with My Husband?

It's interesting that we often find out about the lasting benefits of our mindfulness practice from others. It's not uncommon for a new meditator, just as they're wondering if all this time on the cushion is really working, to have a co-worker, partner or family member comment that they seem nicer, more confident and less easily agitated.

As I revealed in Chapter One, My Rough Road to Mindfulness, when I finally got home from my six-month editing gig in Montreal after leaving *Border Wars*, my number one priority was to repair my tattered marriage. At this point it was a union that had barely survived my being embedded with police agencies at the border for four years.

There were two big problems vis-à-vis my marriage and *Border Wars*. The first, as I previously noted, was that I was rarely home while producing the series. The second may have been worse. Even when I *was* home for one or two weeks between trips, I wasn't *really* home. I was distracted by the endless details and deadlines of my ongoing job and barely present with my wife. As you know, I was also not great at transitioning gracefully from the adrenaline of the production to the slower pace of domestic life.

My wife of 25 years works as a psychotherapist from a home office. She dwells in the inner world while I was very much in the outer world. Our situations at that time were not a good match. When I returned from making *Border Wars*, when I was physically at home, I felt like I had jumped directly from a Blackhawk right into my kitchen. Much to my surprise I was suddenly living with a person who couldn't chase and arrest people, shoot high-definition video or record sound; and who also, as the third and fourth years began to blur together, was becoming a lot less enthusiastic about my gig.

To make matters worse, she was getting very used to living alone and so all my presence did was disrupt her routines. She grew more and more impatient with me, which was confusing because, at work, I was treated with the utmost respect. As she grew tired of my psychological distance, I grew tired of her criticisms. Our precious time at home became so fraught with disagreements that I looked forward to returning with my crewmates to the border zone. It was bad.

To refresh the story from Chapter One, when I finally wrapped up my four-year stint with *Border Wars*, I'd been away from home most of that time. Despite that, I took a job in Canada and went away *again*, for another six months. One reason I took the gig was that we needed the income, but I also feared that if I went home, my wife and I would keep fighting till we broke up. Our marriage was hanging by the thinnest of threads.

Six weeks after I moved to Montreal, to a tiny apartment paid for by the production company, I was in very bad shape. Alone, depressed and anxious, I felt like I was faking my way through my new job. Luckily, no one there had ever met me before and so didn't know the old happier Nick to compare to this new sad Nick. They were none the wiser and in fact, quite welcoming. I thought I could get by as long as I didn't completely fall apart.

That was the bad news. The good news is that this is when I began meditating. As mentioned earlier, I met weekly via Skype with my psychotherapist, Stephen Johnson, Ph.D., a brilliant shrink and the author of an important book entitled *The Sacred Path: The Way of the Spiritual Warrior.*

Dr. Johnson was the first one to tell me about mindfulness, but when he initially mentioned it, I was wholly skeptical and resistant to his counsel. Thank God his tenacity paid off and I finally walked into downtown Montreal and bought Jon Kabat-Zinn's seminal book on mindfulness, *Full Catastrophe Living: Using the Wisdom of Your Body and Mind to Face Stress, Pain, and Illness.*

I read the first two chapters and embarked on a seven-day meditation trial before committing to an ongoing practice. When, after that week I could feel a real positive shift brewing, I kept going. Soon I was like a kid in a candy store. I started reading books by superb mindfulness teachers such as Jack Kornfield, Tara Brach and Joseph Goldstein. I was also listening to podcasts about secular mindfulness, watching TED talks and looking at everything I could find on YouTube.

A few weeks into it I found a meditation group to join. It was made up of both French and English speaking locals. Every Saturday afternoon I would ride my secondhand bike to a local church and it was in their common room that we'd gather, sit, meditate and share. Amazingly, my meditation practice had now helped me find a community of thoughtful and lovely people in a foreign country. I hoped that my restoration was finally at hand.

By Thanksgiving of 2012, the Canadian gig was up. So it was with real trepidation that I returned to my home in Los Angeles. But this time I knew from my practice that I had to really *be* home. I had to be truly present in the moments that my wife and I shared. I had to learn to listen, to inquire about her work and her inner life. I could no longer tune out what I didn't want to hear. I had to be all in, committed to the marriage and take nothing for granted. In short, I had to make her the object of my attention (and affection) whenever we were together. It paid off.

While it was not all smooth sailing, we did have a lot of heart-to-heart talks about what had gone wrong. After about two months of being home – which was now seven months into my meditation practice – the most wonderful thing happened. One evening my wife and I were preparing to leave the house when, out of the blue and apropos of nothing, she turned to me and said, "Ok, who are you and what have you done with my husband?"

I wasn't sure, but I suspected that this was a compliment so I played along and said, "You mean where's *Dick*?" "Yeah," she said, "Where's *Dick*?" "Well, it's hard to say," I answered, "He could show up again anytime, but I'm glad you seem to be happier now with Nick." "Yes, much happier," she said. And then I got the best kiss I'd had in a long time.

All Things in Moderation

Can we entirely control our mood swings, all the highs and lows we can have in the course of a single day? No – no more than we can control the weather. Can mindfulness help us moderate these fluctuations and mitigate the stomach-churning roller-coaster effect? Yes, it can.

One day, I got up early to get to an appointment across town. As I was rushing out the door my now-happier wife reminded me that I had promised to mail an important package for her at the post office. Being singularly focused and in a hurry, I could feel annoyance arising in my body as I began to assign all manner of unflattering characteristics to my beloved. Couldn't it wait till later? No. Did I really say I would do it in the morning? Yes. But what about all the traffic I'd encounter? What if I was late to the meeting? She had two words for me: text them.

This kind of run-of-the-mill conflict used to hold the potential for a high-octane quarrel in the making, but not anymore. While I am not perfect at this, I am much better at taking a couple of deep mindful breaths while sensing the irritation coming up in me. Before angry words could escape my mouth, I grabbed my phone, sent a quick text and went to the post office. My fears were never realized. I was actually just on time, the meeting went well, and everybody got what they wanted.

So again, meditative practice is not a panacea but, generally speaking, the more you meditate, the more familiar you are with your triggers. You've experienced first hand the difference between blind reactivity and a wiser response, and it's your mindfulness that has given you the chance to choose the latter.

A Mind of Its Own

Whatever the origins of our emotions, we often *feel* we have very little control over them. If the phrase, "Your mind's got a mind of its own" resonates with you, it may be because, as John Milton famously wrote in *Paradise Lost*, "The mind is its own place and in itself; [it] can make a Heaven of Hell, a Hell of Heaven."

There is an essential truth in this phrase: that all circumstances are essentially neutral. It's we who make them good or bad. Our brains don't necessarily want to embrace or remember this fact, but it's true.

You step on the scale and it says 190 pounds. That's a fact, but your reaction to it is another whole story – for some, this number would be elation and for others, deep depression. You stub your toe, or get fired from your job and it's the same thing. It happened, now what? You're late to your child's soccer game or you get a diagnosis of kidney disease. Still neutral? Of course.

Circumstances are the tangible *facts* about something; it's called objective reality. The thoughts and the emotions they trigger, on the other hand, are our *response* to those circumstances, and they are, in fact, nothing more than our opinion. Again, it's not a cure-all, but your mindfulness practice can help you realize something important: that every problem that seems like a circumstantial problem *is actually a thought problem.*

Let me repeat that: every problem that seems like a circumstantial problem is actually a thought problem. The day you integrate that idea into your consciousness is the day you start to take control of your life. When we understand that our own interpretations of life situations that determine our feelings, we're on the road to self-determination.

It's Not Your Fault

Taking responsibility for your own unease or unhappiness is far easier said than done, and it's not your fault that this is such a difficult task. Why? As we've discussed before, we're all products of a prehistoric legacy; a brain wired to react emotionally to threats. When translated into our lifetime of conditioning, we're encoded to pay attention to certain aspects of our environment and to ignore others.

Over time we collect mental evidence; file cabinets of habituated assumptions that make it very difficult to see life as it is. The bottom line is this: we make our own reality. We can see the gorgeous sunset, or we can see the "ugly" power lines in our view. We can enjoy an intimate conversation or stop to complain about the airplane noise overhead. Put more simply, "Our life is the creation of our mind," as spoke the Buddha. Or, to quote another sage Eastern thinker, "As you think, so shall you become." (Bruce Lee). It's all well and good to know intellectually that we create our own reality, but knowing this is not enough. We need the ability to *do* something about it.

This is where mindfulness training comes in, as it allows us to increase our objectivity toward the emotional minefield that is our human mind. To take the analogy further, mindfulness is your own minesweeper. With it you can detect the underground potential of what could be an emotional outburst. This allows you to take a deep breath and course correct, thus avoiding more pain and suffering.

That's important because if you can't step back and learn how to observe your moods, thoughts and feelings, you're truly doomed to be lost in them. This whole book is about gaining a modicum of control over your runaway heart and mind. To the degree that you can learn to do it, the happier your day-to-day life will be.

So there it is. Life is a process. It's a long journey. It takes time. Along the way, each occasion where we *intentionally* drop into mindfulness, we've taken another step on a path – the path that's unfolding in every moment.

In this manner your meditation practice can be thought of as a *way*, a way of being, a way of living, a way of loving, and a way of listening. It's a way of walking through life more and more in sync with reality.

CHAPTER 10

THE MINDFUL LANGUAGE OF THE MIND

You know the old saying, "If I had a dime…" Well, if I had a dime for every time someone told me they're not cut out for meditation because they can't stop their racing mind from thinking, I could take my wife out to a really nice lunch with the proceeds.

When that conversation does take place, I just look at them and say, "What do you think *my* mind does? Am I not a human being like you? My mind races all the time, too." The fact is we're all in the same boat and every one of us struggles with a runaway brain. The good news (and something that many people don't know) is that mindful meditation does not ask us to stop *anything*, much less our thoughts because, as we've discussed before, no human can really do that and it's a fool's errand to try.

Mindfulness asks us to observe the mind, and ourselves, exactly as we are at this moment. The thoughts will come, and they will go, and we remain. Yes, we can slow down the "Monkey Mind" by befriending it and following the techniques we've discussed, but stopping or banning your thoughts – no way. You are the observer of thoughts, not the slayer of thoughts.

Mindfulness of the Mind

The simplest way to explain mindfulness of the mind is this: it's the intentional and objective observation of your own mental and emotional self, both in formal meditation and in your daily life. It's the capacity to be present combined with the intention of knowing what's happening in your experience, moment by moment.

When exploring mindfulness of the mind, it's good to make a distinction between your mood (the background "quality" of mind) and mental objects (the foreground contents of mind). Being more awake to your quality of mind means you're cognizant that there's calm or restlessness operating within you; that there's melancholy or gladness, focus or distraction.

It is critical to determine what the inner climate is because this is where your thoughts arise from and, as we all instinctively know, mood will impact everything, from how we think to how we behave.

Did you ever watch a comedy at the movie theater in a lousy mood and find that everyone seems to think it's hilarious but you? In moments like that, you are hyper aware of your mental state, but in other situations someone may have to ask you, "Are you all right?" before you even know there's a problem. I tell my students that mindfulness of mind is akin to knowing your own weather report and, like all things meteorological, it's far better to know what's happening – and what might happen – so as to better "weather" the storms.

Seeing Our Thoughts

So much of mindfulness of mind is learning to become a witness to what we have previously ignored. This is such an important idea; we want to become *aware that we are aware*. Stop and just try that now, let your awareness focus on your awareness…

Use this Acronym: **STOP**

S: Stop whatever you're doing and pause momentarily.
T: Take a breath. Re-connect with your breath. The breath is an anchor to the present moment.
O: Observe. Notice what is happening.
What is happening inside you and outside of you? Where has your mind gone?
What do you feel? What are you doing?
P: Proceed. Continue doing what you were doing. Or don't. Use the information gained during this check-in to maintain or change course. Whatever you do, do it mindfully.

This is why our species is known, technically, as Homo Sapiens Sapiens, which translates to, "Man That Knows and Knows that He Knows."

You never want to take your consciousness for granted, and mindful meditation is key to this fundamental way of functioning. This whole awareness-of-awareness thing is a big deal and a wake-up call to start operating on a whole new plane of reality. Without these intentional and mindful attempts at objectivity, we are slaves to our helter-skelter thoughts and the inevitable reactivity that follows.

Ask yourself this question: is it your mind that decides what you like or don't like, or is it you? It sounds like a funny question to ask but I am serious. With your mind already so conditioned, hardened and opinionated, are you responding to this next moment with any real clarity, curiosity, openness and non-judgment? No? Then you are not nearly as in charge as you think you are.

You Are Not Your Thoughts

Quick. What are you going to think next? You have no idea, so yes, it's a trick question. You *don't* know what thoughts will emerge from your subconscious until the moment they become conscious. You think you authored them, but did you? Think right now about these four things: toast, polar bears, apples and an arrow. What comes next to your mind? You don't know but something will pop up.

By the time you *are* aware of your next idea you're already invested in that thought. You're invested because a lot of unseen effort went into putting it into your mind. The thoughts you have are simply the most robust bits of competing data to win the race from your incognizance to cognizance, soon to be replaced with another winner.

It is very hard *not* to identify with them. And why not – they do seem to be yours, they appear to befit the situation, and they do appear to be rather important, at least to you. But remember, with nearly 70,000 thoughts a day popping up in your head – a rumble in the jungle of past, present and future thinking – you have no more control about what's coming next than a windshield can predict the next bug that will collide with it on the highway.

Fun House Mirror

So your thoughts are less dependent on you than you thought. Let me suggest that your beliefs about what's real and true may be a little suspect as well. We think our mind reflects reality back to us like a big, flat, polished mirror, but I propose that it may be more like a fun-house mirror you'd find at a carnival – you know, the one that shows you with a tiny head and a huge ballooning body. That's not how you really look and you know it immediately.

But when you approach the next person, situation, condition or moment, admit to yourself that your biases, opinions and attitudes are baked into your perceptions. If you are honest you'll admit that your mirror is not big, flat, polished or accurate, so you need some mindfulness for a dose of healthy skepticism about our, true objectivity – or lack of it. Bottom line: the next time you're gazing into that mirror, don't assume you're *not* at the carnival.

One last thought here. The world, in a sense, doesn't really exist out *there*. It's a gazillion pieces of data that pour into you in real time while your brain scrambles to make sense of it using your stored experiences; your memories. Following that process, it's your mind that "reads" the brain's report and decides what to think, say or do – and all of this happens in an instant.

Attention is Reality

Here's another thing to ponder. Your reality is actually based on what you pay attention to, right? Of those gazillion pieces of information that enter your mind through your five senses – like the telephone poles you see rushing by as you drive, or the faces that pass you on a busy sidewalk – most of that information passes right through you.

You see it but you don't really see it. You may barely sense it. In fact, it's so neutral that it's all but invisible to you. But let's say you *do* suddenly recognize a face in the crowd and it's an old girlfriend that you still care about. Suddenly your attention is riveted. That data hits you hard as your memories, emotions and thoughts explode. Or let's say you witness a couple yelling and fighting on the street and it reminds you of your parents fighting. Watch what comes up for you then.

Speaking of relationships, let's say you are getting married tomorrow. The wedding will be outdoors in your parents' backyard, so you go outside the house to look up at the weather. Despite the official weather report calling for a dry, partly sunny day for your big day, you see clouds above and start to get worried. What you *don't* see (even though they are visible to you) are the tall trees, the newly mowed grass, the well-cut hedges and birds in the birdbath. You're only paying attention to the unreliable stories you are telling yourself about the future. Your actual reality is not your actual reality; it's your own rushing thoughts creating an alternate scenario founded on your worry. Welcome to the human race!

Try this: observe, right now, how you're feeling. Let's say that there's restlessness and some agitation coming up for you. See it and feel it but do your best not to form an opinion about it; simply observe.

Now frame your observation as: "There's some agitation here now" rather than "I am agitated." Or if there's anger you might say, "This is my anger coming up again," instead of "I am angry!" The difference is profound; by saying *I am angry* you and your feelings have now been conflated. You and the anger are suddenly the same thing.

But they are *not* the same thing. You are *you,* and your feelings of anger are like a passing thunderstorm of emotions. As we discussed once before, you can't even stay angry for more than a few minutes without your mind throwing another log onto the fire. Each log is just the justification for your anger as you continually revisit the story of what happened. Please note: mindfulness will not keep you from getting angry, but it *can* shorten the life of the angry state. It can stop the emotional bleeding and bring you back to a cooler and more sensible place, and that can make all the difference in the world.

A Parade of Thoughts

If you are a big fan of tortured metaphors (as I clearly am), let's liken your thoughts to the annual Macy's Thanksgiving Day parade. As we've come to expect, this year's parade looks a *lot* like last year's, just as your most pressing thoughts today are much the same as they were yesterday.

Being a veteran of this event, you'll recognize marching bands, colorful dancers, the Rockettes of Radio City Music Hall, Santa (of course), and famous giant balloon characters like Snoopy, Homer Simpson and that enormous turkey. These floating behemoths don't drift away because large groups of hardy handlers (90 per balloon!) keep them tethered to the ground.

Now imagine your own parade of thoughts on a typical day. Like the Macy's parade it's full of captivating and loud, but mostly unimportant, distractions accompanied by a few huge-turkey-balloon-problems that you focus on. The truth is that you let that big turkey into your mind over and over again without even knowing it. You're way past analyzing it, but this huge bird remains an inflated rumination.

And just like the grounds-crew on 7th Avenue, you're employing a lot of mental muscle power to hold it in place. However, if you employ your mindfulness practice to help you release it, you might well see that turkey fly away!

What I hope you'll realize is this: that of the thousands of thoughts you're entertaining each day, precious few have anything to do with the present moment or your immediate concerns. When you start to pay attention to where your attention is actually going, you'll see those marauding and wildly random thoughts appear from nowhere to swoop down, highjack your focus and drag it away. Your precious attention has been kidnapped and taken on a forced march to participate in one haphazard storyline after another.

When this happens (and it does many times daily), that's the time to ask yourself an important question. Are you actually marching *in* the parade without knowing it (in which case it looks just like a normal Thursday to you) or are you able to step back onto the sidewalk and watch the parade go by, seeing it for the madcap cavalcade that it is? If and when you can do that, please don't beat yourself up for hosting the parade in the first place. Instead just smile, be glad you woke up to the truth, and shake your head at your human condition. The bottom line is that mindfulness can help you enjoy the parade…and not be a turkey in it!

Leaning into the Pain

As you may recall, when I began my practice I was desperate for relief but skeptical about meditation. Little had worked to relieve my depression for months and, with my marriage and career on life support, I was not at all optimistic. The inside of my mind was so scary and out of control that I decided to commit to this exotic scheme for just one week. The plan was to meditate ten to twenty minutes per day for seven straight days. If after one week I didn't see any improvement, I'd just quit.

When I began to meditate it was very painful to sit quietly and go inside. What I saw was just how twisted my mind had become. But as I peered into this quagmire of sadness, doubt and self-criticism, this time I didn't turn away. I knew this was my only chance to avert the dissolution of my marriage, my profession and my life. During those seven days I had to face my mind with all its inner demons and I did so unblinkingly. I decided not to use guided meditations, opting instead to rest in complete silence.

This idea of leaning into the pain is a hallmark of mindful meditation and it's the number one reason that maintaining a strong practice, through good times and bad, is so important. When things are mostly okay in your life, your inner GPS can keep you on track, but when your world flips upside down, your meditation practice becomes a life raft.

I know folks who say, "I am too upset to meditate right now. I'll wait till I calm down and then do it." Waiting to be calm in order to meditate is like waiting to call the fire department to come to your burning house until after the fire is out. The time you need to meditate is precisely when you *are* upset. Think about it. You don't wait to calm down in order to meditate; you meditate in order to calm down!

Is it easy to do? Hell, no! Is it extremely useful? Hell, yes! As you sit with the discomfort of whatever has you tied up in knots, you can learn to lean into it with your full attention, whether it's back pain, heartache, anxiety or worse. You try to feel it directly, without a lot internal commentary. You feel it as energy passing up and through you. If you try this with conviction, you'll begin to sense that this intolerable pain is not what it's cracked up to be. On the contrary, it's far more dynamic and malleable than your idea of it.

Let's say you have searing pain in your back, but you decide to zoom in and focus your attention in on it anyway. This is entirely counterintuitive as you'd much rather run away from the pain. It takes considerable courage to lean into the pain but it goes hand-in-hand with embracing the present moment no matter what's going on. As you lean in, you begin to see that the pain is *not* the thing you perceived it to be. It's a series of dynamic sensations that go beyond your mind's opinion of it.

It's not that "damn backache" so much as it's a collection of physical sensations that change constantly. Amplitude and frequency, dullness and sharpness, hot and cold, rough and smooth, it's a shifting phenomenon. This is when you say to yourself, "It's like this right now." What you are attempting is not to make the pain go away. It's about changing your relationship to the pain. It's about realizing that it's only pain if you decide it is. There's a lot to truth to the saying "pain is inevitable but suffering is optional."

Mental Pain

As my meditation practice took hold back in 2012, I began to see that this low-pressure zone I lived in was really just one huge weather front; a long series of intense but passing storms that would eventually end. Today I know that the worst-case scenarios I constantly repeated to myself were neither accurate nor predictive. Slowly I began to grasp that they were only as powerful as my belief in them. In other words, when we believe we are our thoughts, we are tossed about at the whim of every cerebral upset and emotion. A more liberated view comes only when we recognize that thoughts and emotions arise and fall away as part of a process, like breathing.

This realization can inspire self-compassion as we forgive ourselves for being human. As I incorporated this philosophy into my own practice, I was slowly able to find some peace amid the storm. On the sixth day of my weeklong experiment I began to see a subtle shift. I finally gained some desperately needed objectivity toward my persistently negative thoughts. I realized that I didn't have to believe everything that flashed through my mind. This allowed for a detectable shift away from despair and toward hope. It was just enough for me to keep going. I haven't stopped since.

CHAPTER 11

ABSTRACT NOUNS, PART ONE: CONCENTRATION

Think back to elementary school. For many of us it was a rollercoaster of growth spurts and awkward social interactions, all while trying to make decent grades. But with the innumerable trials and errors of grade school there was at least one indisputable grammatical fact: a noun is a person, a place or a thing.

My takeaway from this lesson was that all nouns are concrete things that we can see, hear, smell, taste or touch. Think mountain, foghorn, perfume, scrambled eggs and Velcro. These are all real things in the real world, making it easy for a young mind to understand what a noun is. It was only when we progressed into higher-level classes that we discovered what a truly limited explanation that was.

There are plenty of nouns that do not represent a person, a place or a thing. They are called *abstract* nouns and they refer to things that are not material. Your five physical senses cannot detect abstract nouns; you can't see, smell, taste, hear or touch them. In essence an abstract noun is a quality, a concept, an idea.

Think of it this way; something that is abstract exists only in the mind while something that is material can be interacted with in a physical way. Qualities, relationships, theories, and states of mind are all examples of abstract nouns. Things like love, anger, fear, joy, excitement, courage, bravery or cowardice. Here are a few in context:

We want to see *justice* served.

I'd like the *freedom* to travel all over the world.

Joe felt a nagging sense of *doom.*

When Sally ran into the ocean to rescue a distressed swimmer, her *bravery* astonished onlookers.

Through this chapter and the next two, I will introduce you to three abstract nouns that have a strong connection to a mindfulness practice: *Concentration, Cultivation and Contemplation.* Taken together, these three C's act as a framework that can hold many aspects of our practice.

Concentration

Some of this may sound familiar to you from earlier chapters, but as I have found in my own education, certain foundational ideas must be revisited to truly sink in. This is one of those ideas.

The objective of concentration in terms of mindfulness is using it to deepen your focus. The various techniques under the heading of Concentration Meditation teach you to train your attention on a single object referred to as an anchor. By returning your runaway attention to the chosen anchor, you develop the ability to slow down and become calm and grounded.

Focusing on a single anchor doesn't mean it has to be the same anchor each time. You can take the classic route and follow the inhalation and exhalation of the breath. Or you might focus on other physical sensations arising from your hands, knees, face or your bottom's contact with the chair. You might repeat simple words to yourself, stare at a candle flame or listen to ambient sounds or meditative music. All of them serve the same purpose: to bring your wandering mind back to the here and now.

How to Gather a Scattered Mind

Matthew A. Killingsworth and Daniel Gilbert, the two Harvard psychologists we met in Chapter Three, used cell phone technology to gain insights into the human mind. They developed an iPhone app that contacted 2,250 volunteers at random intervals during the day to ask what they were doing, how happy they were and whether they were actually thinking about their current activity and environment or something else.

Their results revealed that most people spend around 47 percent of their waking hours thinking about something *other than what they're actually doing.* To make matters worse, this mental meandering typically makes them unhappy. "A human mind is a wandering mind, and a wandering mind is an unhappy mind," Killingsworth and Gilbert wrote. "The ability to think about what is *not* happening is a cognitive achievement that comes at an emotional cost."

They go on to say that unlike other animals, humans spend almost half their time contemplating events that have happened in the past, might happen in the future, or will never happen at all. In fact, this kind of distraction appears to be the human brain's default mode of operation. This means that for much of our lives we are anywhere but *here*, living in any time but *now*!

That's an amazing reality check considering that the past is gone and the future is pure speculation. This doesn't mean that we *shouldn't* remember or anticipate things. We must routinely visit the past and future in order to navigate the world in the present, but it's a matter of degree. If we almost *never* return to what's happening here and now, we are literally missing the most important moments of living at all. This is what we mean by walking around on autopilot, continually missing the actual moments of our actual lives.

Early Attempts at Concentration

As you sit quietly in meditation you simply return your attention to the anchor – it could be the breath or it could be real-time sounds – every time you wake up to the wandering. Please note, it's not *if* your mind will wander, it's *when* and for how long. Minds wander; that's what they do. But rather than pursuing each random thought, you see it, acknowledge it and when ready release it to return to the anchor. Through this process your ability to concentrate improves.

It all sounds easy enough but the first thing a beginning meditator discovers is that focusing and refocusing the mind on a single object is really hard. When attempting it, you quickly see just how wild and powerful the human mind is. It is after all *your* mind and you want it to obey you. When you finally notice what's really happening, you'll be humbled by its capacity to utterly disobey you.

Think of trying to tame a wild horse. It's a magnificent beast, but little use to you if it runs amok. Be warned: a beginning meditator will find early attempts at stillness quite discouraging but don't be thwarted. Your first conscious confrontation with the distracted mind is insight number one in a long line of important insights.

On or In the Ocean?

Imagine that the vast ocean is our consciousness and our time in the sea is our time in meditation. Now picture two swimmers. One is a snorkeler, the other a scuba diver. The snorkeler paddles along on the surface of the water. While he may enjoy the view, his understanding of the environment is limited. He bobs up and down like a cork, subject to the wind and the waves of his restless mind. After ten minutes he's tired or bored and heads back to the beach.

Contrast him with the scuba diver. She's outfitted with air tanks and a weight belt that allow her to dive far below the surface. A whole new world opens up to her. Her specialized gear is analogous to our concentration techniques, allowing her to dive deeper. At this depth she's protected from the wind and waves and can stay underwater longer with less effort. Without this level of training and equipment she would simply skim the surface like the snorkeler. The equipment she carries is akin to our powers of focused and concentrated attention.

The Meditative Breath

I had an amazing mindfulness teacher once, Jerome Front, who offered a brilliant 40-minute guided meditation that examined every exquisite and nuanced aspect of a single breath. Beginning at the edge of our noses he led us step by step on a journey past the nostrils, through the nasal cavity, down the windpipe to the moving diaphragm and, on a deeper breath, the filling up of our lungs – and that was just the in breath! Observing all this at a granular level is akin to using an electron microscope to look at your fingerprint. If you did, you'd see the tiny circular ridges of skin that, albeit on a far different scale, are reminiscent of the Grand Canyon!

Experts believe that the practice of meditation can make the breath easier to access in difficult situations. When we get stressed out we tense up and start taking shallow breaths, reducing the amount of oxygen coming in. This causes our bodies to move toward fight-or-flight territory, snowballing into stress and making it hard to calm down. When we relax and breathe more purposefully, we're short-circuiting that negative loop. Let's try this simple breathing exercise and note that it's quite similar to some of our early meditations, which is fine. These concepts, like any new language, require practice and repetition.

EXERCISE: DEEP CONCENTRATION

1. **Find a relaxed, comfortable position**. You can be seated on a chair or a cushion on the floor. Keep your back upright, but not too tight. Hands resting wherever they're comfortable. Close your eyes.

2. **Notice and relax your body**. Try to notice the shape of your body, its weight. Let yourself relax and become curious about your body seated here – the sensations it experiences, the touch and the connection with the floor or chair.

3. **Tune in to your breath**. Feel the natural flow of breathing. In. Out. You don't need to *do* anything to your breath. Not long, not short, just natural. Notice where you feel your breath in your body. It might be in your abdomen. It may be in your chest or throat, or in your nostrils. Feel the sensations, one breath at a time. When one breath ends, sense when the next breath begins.

4. **Be kind to your wandering mind**. As you do this, you will no doubt notice that your mind wanders. You'll start thinking about other things. When this happens it's not a problem. It's natural. Just notice that your mind has wandered and gently redirect your attention back to your breathing.

5. **Stay here for ten minutes**. It may seem like an eternity at first, but set a timer and stick with it. Just keep your attention on your breath, in silence. From time to time you'll get lost in thoughts (mostly stories about the past or future). Don't be dismayed; simply return to your breath.

6. **Check in before you check out**. After a few minutes, once again notice your body, your whole body, seated here. Let yourself relax even more deeply and then offer yourself some appreciation for doing this practice today.

7. **Ding-Ding-Ding.** When the timer rings, open your eyes and go about your day.

Breath Counting Meditation

As we know, breath is the ultimate link between mind and body. Breathing is one of very few physical activities that function both voluntarily and involuntarily. In other words, we can deliberately control it when we think about it, and it happens involuntarily when we don't. Breath counting is a strength-building exercise for the mind. It cleans away distracting thoughts and builds the power of concentration.

EXERCISE: BREATH COUNTING

The first inhale and exhale together count as one. The next inhale/exhale is two. The next full breath (in and out) counts as three, and so on. You will know you're building mental strength when you can easily reach the number 5 and then count back to 1 again without your mind wandering. So that's 1,2,3,4,5 – 5,4,3,2,1.

It sounds pretty easy, right? Try it and see where your mind travels as you do this simple task. Do you think you can count your breaths up to 10 and back to 1? It's a great way to see just how powerful the mind really is. It's a way to find out if you're in charge or if your mind truly has a mind of its own.

Wording: An Alternative Anchor

As we've seen, there are myriad tools and points of focus to enhance our concentration. Breath, sounds, body scans and more. I came up with another one and gave it a name. I call it *wording*, but it is not the same as what wording normally means. Let me explain.

The word *breath* is a noun and the word *breathe* is a verb, but the word *breathing*, depending on its usage, can be either. In the same way the word *wording* is undeniably a noun. It means, "The words used to express something." As in, "His wording of the bad news softened the blow."

Quite on my own, I have decided to make it into a verb, so now *wording* is something you can actually do. In this meditative technique wording is an action and, as the name implies, it uses simple words and phrases to increase concentration.

Please note: Wording is not to be confused with a mantra. Mantras most often come from the ancient languages of Sanskrit or Hindi and are believed to have psychological and spiritual powers. Some are simply used to create an internal vibration (like OM), and others are images and instructions that hearken back to the earliest days of Hinduism.

Wording, on the other hand, uses a few actual words; words that have real meaning. To be effective they need to be simple and flexible. These words are chosen for their different and subtle meanings and are to be used in repetition to foster concentration.

I have embraced this alternative anchor point, *wording*, because for me, concentrating primarily on the breath sometimes is not enough to tame the monkey in my mind. Wording can help solve that problem. What follows are some of my favorite examples of wording, used in conjunction with breathing.

EXERCISE: WORDING

1. As you inhale, silently say to yourself: Just…

Exhale and silently say to yourself: Be…

Now repeat these two words with each complete breath.

Just be; just be; just be; just be…

---

2. As you inhale, silently say to yourself: Here…

Exhale and silently say to yourself: Now…

Now repeat these two words with each complete breath.

Here now; here now; here now…

---

3. As you inhale, silently say to yourself: Let…

Exhale and silently say to yourself: Go…

Now repeat these two words with each complete breath.

Let go; let go; let go…

Concentration is the primary abstract noun of Mindfulness. Now we'll move on to two other critical abstract nouns, *Cultivation* and *Contemplation*.

CHAPTER 12

ABSTRACT NOUNS, PART TWO: CULTIVATION

This chapter explains how meditation and mindfulness can put us on a path toward positive change.

The word I like for this experience is *cultivation* and yes, it's another abstract noun grounded in the notion of nurturing something of value inside ourselves. It describes the process of developing a quality or skill.

Neuroplasticity

Until recently, common knowledge held that people's fundamental natures really don't change; that their basic personalities were fixed at an early age. Whatever characteristics they possessed were not subject to alteration as they grew older. However, in the last 15 years, neuroscientists have discovered that our brains are surprisingly malleable as we age. It turns out that while our early life temperament provides a strong baseline, it doesn't tell the whole story.

The formal name for this malleability is neuroplasticity, which describes the ongoing changes in our neural pathways that occur due to interactions with information, behavior and environment. As we experience life, the brain engages in what's called *synaptic pruning*. Neural connections that are no longer useful are deleted, while necessary ones are strengthened.

This is a very exciting concept, confirming that our brains continue to evolve throughout our lives. Even more exciting is the fact that we can consciously promote the scope and rapidity of these alterations by stimulating our minds. As it turns out, meditation is an extremely valuable tool to keep our brains growing and changing in very beneficial ways.

Cultivation

We all know that mindfulness is growing in popularity and it's no wonder. It's a safe, natural and cost-effective way to improve our mental and emotional health. With this new level of social acceptance, people recognize that the value of the practice goes far beyond just benefiting ourselves. As we become calmer, kinder, and more focused, we affect the folks around us: coworkers, family and friends.

As I teach it, the word *cultivation* has two meanings. The first has to do with cultivating specific qualities that we perceive as desirable. Happiness, empathy, kindness, patience and resilience are not necessarily gifts that we're born with. Enhancing these virtues in ourselves turns out to be a trainable skill set, but like any other skill, it's something we must work on. This idea is at the core of the first book in this series, Valerie Alexander's *Happiness as a Second Language.*

The second meaning of *cultivation* is practical. It addresses the creation of optimal conditions for a solid meditation practice. We've already discussed how the trickiest part is just showing up and sitting down. Indeed, carving out time and space to get onto the cushion is 95% of a winning strategy.

It won't surprise you then that the first meaning of cultivation is supported by the second. How's that? Cultivating a strong practice gives you the chance to cultivate a better you. That being said, there are specific meditations that do this.

A Cultivation Prayer

Before I get into some of the meditations I use, here's one you may be very familiar with. It's a well-known Christian cultivating meditation called the Serenity Prayer, written by the American theologian, Reinhold Niebuhr. This prayer has become one of the most widely known invocations in the world, as it touches peoples' hearts from all cultures regardless of religious affiliation.

God, grant me the serenity to accept the things I cannot change, courage to change the things I can, and wisdom to know the difference.

The intention of the Serenity Prayer is to ask your higher power for the wisdom to gracefully acknowledge what *is* – meaning, what cannot be changed by us. It also asks us to recognize when action is necessary for things that can be changed. This prayer expresses the Buddhist understanding of equanimity and acceptance, which are two notions that lie at the heart of that philosophy. Like mindfulness, the Serenity Prayer directs you to live in each moment even as you embrace the inevitable struggles and challenges of life.

Cultivating Loving Kindness

Perhaps one of the most healing things we can do for others and ourselves is to cultivate love, kindness and compassion. The first technique I'll show you is as old as the Buddha and as new as 21st century neuroscience.

Researchers have tested the outcomes of this practice, which is called Loving Kindness Meditation, or LKM, in fMRI (functional MRI) brain scanning machines. The brains of novice, intermediate and veteran meditators practicing LKM are monitored inside these high-tech tubes, and researchers can see exactly what is activated in the brain when a person wishes themselves and others well.

Loving Kindness Meditation is exactly what it sounds like. It uses repeated words that focus on enhanced feelings of goodwill, kindness and compassion. You can wish for happiness for yourself and your family and friends of course – but you also need to include good wishes for people you don't know and people you don't like. It's important that you, on occasion, try to do this word-based meditation for even your worst enemy.

Warning: when you first try LKM, the meditation might seem a bit too precious, too syrupy, maybe too New Age. I know because that's how it felt to me when I was introduced to it. It made me feel self-conscious at first, but with ongoing practice, it grew on me. Today I trust it to alter my consciousness and re-frame my outlook. Let me tell you how LKM helped me in my life.

After a dispute over the disposition of properties that my father left us, one of my siblings and I had a painful falling out and didn't talk to each other for about a year. When I meditated during that time, I used LKM to soften my heart and wish them well. To be clear, I was not engaging in magical thinking, nor was I testing my powers of ESP. The other person had no idea I was doing this. This meditation affects the meditator, not the recipient, as it softens one's own heart. It allowed me to think about the love I've had for this person my whole life and it ultimately allowed me to forgive and move on.

When you're really upset with someone, have you noticed that you start engaging in long conversations with them that exist only in your own head? Have you heard the saying that the anger you hold onto is like drinking poison while expecting the other person to die? I know that LKM works as it helped me restore my relationship with that sibling.

S.H.E.I.L.A.

A woman named Sheila has participated in my monthly meditation class for five years now and, as a bonus for all of us, she even volunteered to help proofread and edit this book! Her dedication to the practice inspired me to create an LKM using her name as an acronym.

Please note again, we can do this "prayer" for ourselves as well as all manner of other people. We often start with a person we might call a benefactor. This is someone we love unconditionally. As soon as we think of them, we sincerely want the very best for them. From there we widen our scope by bringing to mind and naming family members, good friends and co-workers. As the circle of light gets wider still you can send loving kindness to acquaintances like your mail carrier or a barista in your local coffee shop.

As the circle widens further you include people you don't much care for, people who annoy you and really push your buttons. This last part is *really* hard, but you'll be amazed how you can find compassion even for these people.

With a world population of almost eight billion, you know full well that these people did not come into this life just to torture you. They are complex creatures just as you are. They are products of their upbringing as well. They have had their share of abuse and sorrow as well. They may have many of the same problems, fears and insecurities as you do, but along the way they maladapted to them. Again, this is a chance to soften *your* heart and keep you from holding on tightly to any judgment or narrow view you have. Read the meditation below and then try it for yourself. *I* means you, *we* means a community of people you belong to, and *they* means a 3rd party individual or group.

S = May (I, we, they) be Safe and free from danger.

H = May (I, we, they) be as Happy and Healthy as possible.

E = May (I, we, they) know Equanimity and Ease, and be at peace.

I = May (I, we, they) know the importance of Impermanence.

L= May (I, we, they) give and receive Love in equal measure.

A = May (I, we, they) appreciate being Awake, Aware and Alive.

Now that you've sampled it, perhaps you feel it's a bit too syrupy for you, kind of like a Buddhist Hallmark card. I get it. But with practice you'll feel the power of it. It really does change the energy, turn down the volume, soften the heart and promote good will. It allows you to down-regulate your own nervous system and feel better.

Loving Kindness Meditation is just one of many meditation practices that seek to cultivate qualities that help us become more compassionate people.

"Just Like Me" Meditation

Another cultivation meditation is a cousin to LKM and is called the *Just Like Me* meditation. When you try this one, invoke someone you're in conflict with, be it a slight disagreement or a full-blown feud.

The idea here is that the more we perceive someone as being similar to ourselves (just like me), the more likely we are to feel and act positively towards that person. As in LKM, kind and empathetic thoughts, with practice, help you form healthy mental habits. The end result is that you suffer less and your relationships improve. I have found the *Just Like Me* practice to be tremendously helpful in healing a variety of relationships.

For instance, whenever I was in a conflict with somebody at work, I would often leave the office and walk around the block. After I'd sufficiently calmed down, I would recollect that person in my mind and do the exercise below. By the time I was done, at least half my anger was gone. It's a very useful practice, both at home and at work.

First, picture the person who will be the object of the meditation. Imagine they are right in front of you. Remember that he or she is a fellow flawed human being, just like you. Now close your eyes and say these phrases to yourself.

JUST LIKE ME MEDITATION

Just Like Me this person is imperfect.

Just Like Me this person gets misunderstood and frustrated.

Just Like Me this person has been sad, angry and confused.

Just Like Me this person deals with difficult feelings and thoughts.

Just Like Me this person has experienced physical pain.

Just Like Me this person has experienced emotional pain.

Just Like Me this person wants to be free from pain and suffering.

Just Like Me this person wants to be happy.

Just Like Me this person wants to be safe, healthy and loved.

Cultivating Gratitude

Too often we find ourselves caught up in the difficulties of our lives and can only see what's wrong in and around us. We get bogged down with the challenges we face, and sometimes find it easier to focus on the negative than on the positive. This is perfectly natural and is hard-wired into us by evolution. It's a survival instinct to always be on the lookout for threats to our wellbeing.

Having said that, if you find yourself wanting to steer your thoughts in a more positive direction, then gratitude meditation may do the trick. Research shows that people who regularly practice gratitude experience far more positive emotions. They take the time to notice and reflect upon the things they're thankful for. As a result they feel better, sleep better and express more compassion towards others. There is some evidence that they even have stronger immune systems.

Set a timer for three minutes, find a comfortable, quiet place to sit and think only of things you are grateful for. If you complete your list before the time is up, keep repeating those things you have already thought of.

Cultivating Self-Compassion

A main objective of cultivation meditation is to hone the skill of compassion for oneself. Let's face it, self-compassion does not come naturally to most of us and if we do have it, we rarely use it. In fact, no one is harder on us than we are. We're all very good at self-criticism.

Why? Because that's what we practice. Remember that searing internal heat when you have well-and-truly screwed up? That feeling that the blame is clearly yours, especially when the consequences are not so inconsequential? I've had that experience more times than I wish to admit.

For instance, there was the time I sent that email criticizing a key network TV executive…and copied that executive! And the time I moved my wife's favorite fountain to a new place in the garden and it fell off my hand trolley and broke in half. Then there's the time a friend asked me why I didn't socialize with him and his wife much anymore. "Because I can't stand how she treats you so disrespectfully in public," was my honest answer. That ended our friendship right then and there. I felt terrible but with some self-compassion meditation I began to forgive myself, all the while still sorry that I had hurt him.

Self-compassion is a practice of goodwill, not good feelings. If we use a self-compassion practice simply to ease immediate mental pain, things will only get worse. With self-compassion, we accept that the moment is painful and hold ourselves with kindheartedness, remembering that suffering and imperfection are part of our shared human experience. Here is one approach to a self-compassion meditation.

EXERCISE: SELF-COMPASSION MEDITATION

1. Contemplate a time when you have suffered or recognize your current suffering in real time.

2. Notice how you feel when you think of your suffering. How does it feel in your chest and heart area? Notice the tension in your jaw or shoulders.

3. Just as you would wish for a loved one's suffering to lessen, now wish to ease your own suffering. Try to recognize, allow and investigate it to see it simply as more mental data to respond to.

4. Silently recite to yourself:

- May I recognize my suffering.
- May I allow it, feel it, investigate it.
- May I know it's impermanent.
- May I remember that we all suffer.
- May I forgive myself for my shortcomings.
- May I remember my good qualities.
- May I be kind to myself.
- May I forgive myself.
- May I be free from this suffering.
- May we all be free from suffering.

Stop and notice how this feels in your heart and in the rest of your body. Do you feel different than you did when you wished for the suffering of others to be calmed? Did you feel some tenderness for yourself? Did you begin to forgive yourself for being a fragile and imperfect human with strong emotions and natural reactivity? Making this a part of your practice can take you a long way on your journey to wellbeing.

Cultivating a Sustainable Practice

To remind you, in this teaching the word *cultivation* has two meanings.

We first went through a number of qualities one can cultivate, including kindness, compassion and gratitude; attributes that are of the utmost benefit to ourselves and others. The second kind of cultivation is practical because it addresses the care and maintenance of your new practice.

I talk to a lot of people about their meditation practices and believe me, *everyone* wishes they could be a more consistent meditator. Even those who have never done it feel certain that if they *did* do it, they'd be far more centered and happier. The big question for most people is time. How can they possibly find five, ten or even fifteen minutes to sit alone quietly?

I gently remind them that CEOs of Fortune 500 companies, top athletes and politicians find the time to quietly sit in meditation every day.

In the morning I used to rush around the house, shower, get dressed, grab some food, compare schedules with my wife, answer emails and run out the door. That was then. Now, here's what I do. I get up thirty minutes earlier. I make a cup of tea. I stretch a bit. I sit in my favorite chair. I read a few inspiring passages from one of my favorite mindfulness books and then I meditate for ten to fifteen minutes. I try to do this every day. During this time, I devote myself to being entirely present. I use a variety of concentration techniques to focus my attention on my breath and body, all the while trying to discern the inner workings of my mind.

I don't do this to become a better meditator. I do this in order to: (a) revisit and cherish the inner landscape of my mind and body; (b) recognize how vital this stillness is as a counterweight to endless busy-ness and distractions; and (c) enjoy the resultant benefits of being more and more present in my daily life and with the people I care about.

A Practical Practice

Let's get practical and take a look at some of the real-world ways we can successfully get ourselves to the cushion. These include *when* to meditate, *where* to meditate and *how* to arrange our schedule to make time for this important act of self-care. While it might sound obvious, we all need reminding that meditation only works when we commit to actually doing it.

We all know by now that maintaining a daily meditation practice is easier said than done. With this in mind, here are some tips to help you set yourself up for a regular and consistent meditation practice. I hope this will help to ward off any excuses before they come knocking.

EXERCISE: COMMITTING TO YOUR PRACTICE

1. **How to sit:** Sit on a chair, a couch or on your bed. If you're comfortable on the ground, sit cross-legged. Just sit somewhere quiet and comfortably.

2. **Where to sit:** As you begin to practice more regularly, you can make a special place in your home. Make this your go-to meditation space.

3. **When to sit:** First thing each morning is best, if possible. It's easy to say, "I'll meditate every day," and then forget to do it. Instead, set a reminder for every morning when you get up, and put a note that says "meditate" somewhere where you'll see it.

4. **Prioritize:** If meditating in the morning isn't your bag, make sure that you prioritize it. Remember that nothing is more important than the health of your mind. Program a reminder in your smart phone.

5. **Be flexible:** Be prepared to be flexible with your routine. Not every day is going to look the same, which might mean you have to move your meditation to a different place or time. Be sure to do it before you get too sleepy and don't let work be an excuse to skip it altogether. Even if you meditate for just a few minutes, it's worth it. Remember, frequency beats duration.

6. **Be less judgmental:** Try not to judge your meditation session. There's a natural tendency to rate this as a good or bad meditation. In reality, there is no such thing. All efforts to meditate are good because even when you struggle, you are aware of the power of the mind. If you understand the long-term purpose of your practice, this will never be a problem.

7. **Manage your expectations:** Daily meditation is a life-long skill, not a quick fix solution. While you might see some immediate benefits, others might take longer to appear. Make sure you focus on just taking each day as it comes.

8. **Remind yourself of the benefits:** After each session, make sure you take a moment to notice how you feel – physically, emotionally and mentally. As soon as you start establishing a connection between your meditation practice and feeling better, the easier you will find it to sit down each day and maintain a consistent practice.

There's another element to creating optimal environmental "hacks" that help you get to the cushion. The number one thing to do is create a meditation space in your home. Find a place where you feel immediate calm when you sit. Make this *your* space, a place that offers privacy and yet easy access. Put a few of your favorite items there; things that help you concentrate and get centered. You might have a small table with favorite photos, books, and personal items. You might have a singing bowl or a bell there.

You can also use the buddy system where you have a meditation friend to check in with. Together you can support each other's practices. You don't have to meditate at the same time, but simply having someone who's also looking to establish a strong meditation routine can help spur you on and strengthen your commitment.

CHAPTER 13

ABSTRACT NOUNS, PART THREE: CONTEMPLATION

The last couple of chapters were built on two abstract nouns: *concentration* and *cultivation*. In this way we're erecting a scaffolding to help us build and maintain our practice. We are also preparing the ground for a third abstract noun: *contemplation*. Taken together, *concentration, cultivation and contemplation* (Three C's of Mindfulness) can create a powerful framework to encompass our training.

When I first got serious about my meditation practice, I had absolutely no idea where this journey would take me. At the time I was most concerned with finding my way out of my post-*Border Wars* blues. My symptoms were crushing depression, rampant anxiety and loss of hope that I'd ever feel normal again. I started practicing meditation at the lowest point in my life, so I know, without a doubt, that my practice has been a genuine lifesaver for me. Little did I realize back then that it would also open up a whole new philosophical outlook as well, one that would lead me to ask the most profound questions a person can ponder.

Spirituality

To my way of thinking, the word *contemplation* takes us into the more philosophical, if not spiritual, aspects of our training. What do I mean by spiritual, especially given that we're learning a decidedly secular approach to our meditation practice? Spirituality is a broad concept with room for many perspectives. In general, I think it includes a heartfelt sense of connection to something bigger than us; some way of knowing there's more to being human beings than just our sensory experience. It's a search for meaning in this brief, chaotic and random human experiment. Meditation checks these boxes as it helps you, over time, divine your place in the fabric of life writ large.

When we meditate, we tap into the brain-body connection we inherited from our ancestors. As we inquire within, we naturally come to ask why we are here, both as a species and as individuals. This implicit search is native in all of us, whether we're hardcore atheists, undecided agnostics or devoutly religious. To meditate in this context is to seek an inner vision, one that's beyond the intellect.

The time you spend in the stillness of formal meditation is itself a profound act of introspection. I said it before and I'll say again, as you pause to look deeply into *your* nature, you are looking into the larger truth of *human* nature. Your body and mind have the same needs as do all human bodies and minds. We have physical needs such as air, water, nutrients, shelter and sleep, but we also need the inner sustenance of certainty, variety, significance, love, and connection.

When we feel a lack in any of these areas, we overcompensate in ways that are neurotic and we suffer. Mindfulness asks you to view yourself with compassion, knowing that being human means to suffer and have flaws. The more you accept the truth of that, the more you accept yourself with all your foibles. As I am fond of saying, "Being human: it's not your fault, it's just your turn!"

The Voice in your Head

Quickly and silently, think of your full name.

Now your home address.

OK, now silently describe your home.

Do you hear the voice?

What language is it speaking?

Do you recognize it as the same voice that yammers at you all day long?

Once you really hear it, you must then ask yourself this profound question: who the hell is listening?

If there's a speaker, it naturally follows that there's a listener. Are there two of you? Are you the voice or are you the witness to the voice? In the same way, are you your thoughts and emotions or are you simply the recipient of these perceptions, with very little control over their rising and fading away? It's all worth asking.

How is it that you "hear" your inner voice? Chances are, as you're reading this sentence, you're listening to your inner voice right now. The language is coming to you from *my* words, but it's generated in *your* head. In psychological jargon this voice is called internal, or inner, speech.

Sometimes it's referred to as self-talk. Internal speech uses the same decoding system that we employ for processing external language, which is why we understand a voice that no one else can hear. Inner speech allows us to describe our own lives to ourselves and, like a narrator's voice-over in a documentary film, it tends to be a bit redundant with the visual information we're already taking in.

For instance, I might find a missing sock when doing the laundry. I see the sock; I immediately understand its significance – and yet I'm compelled to say to myself, "Oh, there it is. Good. I wondered where it was. It's so darn easy to lose one sock." Clearly no one's around to hear this fascinating dialogue (thank goodness!) and just as clearly, I realize that it's not really necessary to have this conversation at all. But guess what, we can't help it; it's an automatic brain feedback loop and we're stuck with it forever.

Imagine if all your internal speech was somehow wired to a loudspeaker, like my drum instructor's amplified heartbeat, and everyone near you was privy to these conversations in your skull. They'd hear all of the mundane, bizarre, silly, nonsensical and scary parts of your endless narrative. They would no doubt conclude that you're either the world's most boring person, or just plain nuts. The good news is that by learning the language of Mindfulness, you can become more cognizant of how of your internal monologues work, and then give thanks that these inner chats are 100% private.

The Big Questions

As we continue to meditate, we increasingly find ourselves asking the big questions. Who am I? Am I my name, my thoughts, my ever-changing body? Am I my memories or the various roles I play in this life? What's the true nature of my identity? Where is the "I" who says "I am?"

When we go in search of ourselves, is there a self to find? Where exactly does the thinker of our thoughts reside and who is listening to all of our ceaseless self-talk? Are we some *thing* or are we instead a dynamic, ever-changing process?

There are so many profound issues to explore in our practice. What is the genesis of our emotions? Where is the root of our compassion, hatred, love, anger, greed and delusion? Why do we suffer, grow old, get sick and die? What is enlightenment and is it possible to achieve?

As our practice grows deeper, we might wonder about this: what is the difference between objective truth and subjective reality? Can we ever really know the veracity of anything? Does fate exist or is everything totally random?

Perhaps the biggest question of them all is this: what's the true purpose of our time here on this planet? I didn't expect to be asking these imponderables when I started my meditation practice but it came with the territory.

The Hard Problem and The Comfort Zone

When we contemplate the idea of consciousness, we might describe it as awareness of ourselves and our environment. Another way to put it is this: to be truly self-aware you have to not only think your thoughts but understand that you're thinking those thoughts. This goes to the heart of mindfulness; to cultivate enough stillness and objectivity to know and know that you know.

Despite centuries of exploration, the nature and even the existence of consciousness remains inscrutable and controversial, being at once the most fundamental and most mysterious feature of our lives. It's been dubbed *the hard problem* because it is the problem of consciousness itself, as in, what is it and where is it?

With our mindfulness practice we get to be amateur detectives trying to solve the hard problem firsthand as we deconstruct and probe what it's truly like to have a subjective experience – what it's like to be yourself in this precise moment. As you sit quietly and go within, you are beginning the process of becoming aware of your own awareness.

In our daily lives we're certainly not sitting around pondering the mysteries of consciousness. Most of the time we are just trying to stay comfortable. Our own comfort zone is of primary importance to us whether it's our physical comfort, emotional comfort or intellectual comfort. We shift in our chair, we adjust the temperature, and we change the channel. When outside, we wear sunglasses, pull our collar up and stroll while listening to our favorite music. We fine-tune everything to feel as good as we can in each moment. In fact, the largest percentage of our time is spent trying to figure out what will make us happier, even if just for the next few moments.

On the flip side, if you look at your life honestly, you'll see just how quickly you can become dissatisfied with things you thought you wanted. Alas, we are always looking for the next new thing. The next meal, the next TV show, the next job or even the next romantic partner.

Mother nature has always rewarded us for seeking out pleasure rather than pain; this helps to ensure that we're recurrently unsatisfied, condemned to eternally want things to be new, different and fresh. We always want a little less or a little more. If we want it, we want it now. If we don't want it, it can't leave soon enough!

The bottom line is this: natural selection did *not* evolve to make us happy. Evolution really does not care that we're content, its only job is to make sure we pass our DNA down through the ages. You may remember that this is what the Buddhists mean by *dukkha*.

This word is from the ancient Pali language and it's an important Buddhist concept. As you'll recall from the start of this book, *dukkha* commonly translates as *suffering*, but it can also mean *unsatisfactoriness*. Much of Buddhist doctrine is based on the fact that all human beings inevitably suffer, in small and mundane ways as well as big and existential ways.

Dedicated Buddhists thus study the reality, the cause, and the tools for mitigating or even extinguishing this suffering. We who teach secular mindfulness are following in their ancient steps. This is where contemplation serves you. When you become deeply contemplative, you can expand your full understanding of, and thus lessen, all human suffering, and principally, your own.

CHAPTER 14
FINAL THOUGHTS

As you think back on this book, I want you to remember that the map is not the territory. What makes up all these chapters are merely words that point to a direct, embodied experience.

As I wrote them, I was offering you an *idea* about what the practice is, but to become truly fluent in Mindfulness, you must have an honest and sustained encounter with it for yourself. If you are interested in using this book as a launching pad for your own practice (and I fervently hope you are), please be sure to use the resource list in Chapter 15. It will point you to apps and books, magazines, podcasts and videos.

If Not Now, When?

I am writing this last chapter in September of 2020, which means I am wrapping up this book in the time of the

Covid-19 Pandemic and inconceivably destructive wildfires across the western United States. For almost six months now, my wife and I have been in serious lockdown mode and now we have a city full of smoke to deal with as well.

Of course, there are millions of essential workers who are still risking their lives and health to make sure the lights stay on and the food supply continues. A partial list of those amazing people includes healthcare providers and caregivers, first responders and public safety officers, essential workers in the energy sector, food service, public works and infrastructure services and many, many more.

Millions are out of work as the world waits for a safe and affordable vaccine. To say that there's never been a better time to establish a robust meditation practice is yet another enormous understatement. If not now, when? We need all the help we can get these days. We need the discipline, the consistency, the resilience and the stress reduction.

We need the calm, the reframing of our worries, the objectivity and the stillness. We need this radical act of self-care more than ever, for ourselves and all the loved ones in our lives.

My wife and I are among the lucky ones. I'm retired from forty years in TV and she's able to do her work from home, but like so many others, I feel rather helpless these days and I do what I can. My main form of giving back, aside from supporting various charitable efforts, is to run mindfulness and meditation groups via Skype or Zoom technology. It's an honor for me to create a safe place where I can offer these tools in a time of great stress and uncertainty.

As we all know, it doesn't take a once-in-a-hundred-years pandemic to have your life turned upside down. There are no guarantees that life won't throw you a serious curveball at any moment. It could be the loss of a job or an important relationship; extreme financial hardship; someone's unexpected death, sickness or injury. All of these things can heave us down a black hole of worry and despair.

I tell people that my meditation practice is what keeps my ship afloat while navigating the vagaries of everyday life, but when things get really scary, my daily sitting practice once again becomes a lifeline. I firmly believe that meditation is a powerful benefit in these moments.

Meditation is a critical tool in our tool belt, an invaluable go-to strategy for self-regulation and stress reduction. It's important, especially in times of great anxiety, to find a way home, knowing that you *are* your home. You, your mind and your heart; they are still there waiting for you.

I hope this book has been of help to you. I am here for you and you can always find me through my website – *strategicstillness.com*.

May you be well.

CHAPTER 15

KEY PHRASES IN THE LANGUAGE OF MINDFULNESS

Every book in the *"…as a Second Language"* series ends with a chapter called Key Phrases. The idea is that when you're learning a new language, you need some easy, go-to phrases to return to over and over. It's our own version of, "Donde está la biblioteca?"

What follows are significant quotes from some of the greatest minds of today and the past. These wonderful quotes prove two things:

1. Mindfulness and meditation have been around for a very long time (about 3,000 years).
2. The mindfulness movement is growing exponentially – and more so every day.

Enjoy!

The best way to capture moments is to pay attention. This is how we cultivate mindfulness.

– Jon Kabat -Zinn

Jon Kabat-Zinn is the founder of the Center for Mindfulness at the University of Massachusetts Medical School, where he developed the Mindfulness-Based Stress Reduction program or MBSR.

Meditation is not evasion; it is a serene encounter with reality.

– Thích Nhất Hạnh

Thích Nhất Hạnh is a Buddhist monk, author, and mindfulness teacher who was nominated for the Nobel Peace Prize in 1967 by Dr. Martin Luther King, Jr.

Everything that has a beginning has an ending. Make your peace with that and all will be well.

– Jack Kornfield

Jack Kornfield is a mindfulness teacher and author who (along with Sharon Salzberg and Joseph Goldstein) founded the Insight Meditation Society.

Meditation is not a perk that makes this a nice, fluffy place to work. It makes you better and it makes the company better. We really believe in the hard science aspects of it.

– Evan Williams

Evan Williams is the Co-Founder of Twitter.

Meditation practice isn't about trying to throw ourselves away and become something better. It's about befriending who we are already.

– Pema Chödrön

Pema Chödrön is a Buddhist nun and author who has written several popular books about mindfulness.

Altogether, the idea of meditation is not to create states of ecstasy or absorption, but to experience being.

– Chögyam Trungpa

Chögyam Trungpa was the 11th Trungpa tülku, an important figure in Tibetan Buddhism, and a major influence in introducing Tibetan Buddhism to the West.

Mindfulness isn't difficult, we just need to remember to do it.

— Sharon Salzberg

Sharon Salzberg is a mindfulness teacher and author who (along with Jack Kornfield and Tara Brach) founded the Insight Meditation Society in 1975.

Meditation is like a gym in which you develop the powerful mental muscles of calm and insight.

— Ajahn Brahm

Ajahn Brahm is a British-Australian Buddhist monk.

Thoughts are just that – thoughts.

— Allan Lokos

Allan Lokos is the author of *Patience: The Art of Peaceful Living.*

The only way to live is by accepting each minute as an unrepeatable miracle.

— Tara Brach

Tara Brach, Ph. D. is a clinical psychologist, an internationally known teacher of mindfulness meditation, and author of the bestselling books *Radical Acceptance, True Refuge* and *Radical Compassion.*

If you just sit and observe, you will see how restless your mind is. If you try to calm it, it only makes things worse, but over time it does calm, and when it does, there's room to hear more subtle things — that's when your intuition starts to blossom and you start to see things more clearly and be in the present more.

– Steve Jobs

Steve Jobs was a co-founder of Apple.

In moments of madness, meditation has helped me find moments of serenity – and I would like to think that it would help provide young people a quiet haven in a not-so-quiet world… It's a lifelong gift, something you can call on at any time… I think it's a great thing.

– Paul McCartney

Sir Paul McCartney is a musician and founder of The Beatles.

Do not dwell in the past, do not dream of the future, concentrate the mind on the present moment.

– Buddha

The *Buddha* (also known as Siddhartha Gautama) was a philosopher, meditator, and spiritual teacher who lived in ancient India (c. 5th to 4th century BCE). He is revered as the founder of the world religion of Buddhism.

When meditation is mastered, the mind is unwavering like the flame of a candle in a windless place.

– Bhagavad Gita

The *Bhagavad Gita (Song of God)* is among the most important religious texts of Hinduism and easily the best known.

Be here now. Be someplace else later. Is that so complicated?

– David M. Bader

David M. Bader is a humorist who wrote *Zen Judaism: For You a Little Enlightenment.*

I have lived with several Zen masters – all of them cats.

– Eckhart Tolle

Eckhart Tolle is a spiritual teacher and best-selling author. He wrote the best-selling book, *The Power of Now.*

The mind is definitely something that can be transformed, and meditation is a means to transform it.

– The 14th Dalai Lama.

The 14th Dalai Lama is the current Dalai Lama.

Your vision will become clear only when you look into your heart. Who looks outside, dreams. Who looks inside, awakens.

– Carl Jung

Carl Gustav Jung was a Swiss psychiatrist and psychoanalyst who founded analytical psychology.

APPENDIX
RESOURCE GUIDE

I hope you discovered this guide early on so you've been able to use some of the resources below as you moved through the book. Here you will find an invaluable supply of apps, books, magazines, websites, podcasts and videos.

Meditation may be thousands of years old, but here in the 21st century we are blessed with a cornucopia of extraordinary resources, all just a click away – the greatest mindfulness thinkers, meditation teachers, simpatico groups to join, either live or via videoconference; it goes on and on.

In fact, there are so many choices it can be quite dizzying. I recommend finding an app, book, teacher and/or podcast that feels right and giving it a long audition. There's nothing like consistency when you begin, and I have personally used and vetted every recommendation in this chapter.

I also recommend that you find a good meditation teacher in your area for individual or group work. I have taken more classes than I can remember and have learned from many wonderful teachers. To this day I still avail myself of the best trainers I can find, whether at an all-day meditation seminar, on a multi-day retreat, or by reading a book or listening to an app. For many of us, a four, six or eight session once-weekly course is a great way to jump in. For those just starting, it's amazing how being assigned meditation as your "homework" does wonders for your consistency and discipline.

I hope you've found this book both entertaining and useful. I firmly believe that your newfound practice of mindful meditation will have an enormous positive impact, not only in your life, but also in the lives of everyone around you.

Namaste,
Nick

Definitions of Mindfulness

Paying attention, on purpose, in the present moment, non-judgmentally, for the cultivation of wisdom and compassion.
- Jon Kabat-Zinn

Mindfulness is a state of active, open attention on the present. When mindful, you carefully observe your thoughts and feelings without judging them to be good or bad.
- Psychology Today

Apps

Headspace

Headspace is one of the best-known meditation apps on the market with hundreds of themed sessions on everything from stress and sleep to focus and anxiety.

Calm

Apple's App of the Year in 2017, Calm is a leading app for meditation and mindfulness. It has over 100 guided meditations to help manage anxiety, lower stress and sleep better.

Insight Timer

Entry price: Free, but you have to navigate around the subscription screen with the button that says "Start 7 Day Trial." Once you scroll past that, you can access the free content. Insight Timer has an insanely huge library of content: over 25,000 guided meditations from around 3,000 teachers on topics like stress, relationships, sleep, creativity and more.

Ten Percent Happier

A terrific app created by ABC news reporter and anchorman, Dan Harris, working with a group of phenomenal teachers. Built for everyone, it's perfect for those Dan calls *Fidgety Skeptics*. He was one himself when he first heard about meditation.

Waking Up

Sam Harris (no relation to Dan) is a neuroscientist, philosopher and best-selling author. He explores some of the most important questions about the human mind, society, and current events with extremely interesting guests. This app is his contribution to the field and it's more advanced than the apps above.

YouTube Channels

Wisdom 2.0

Wisdom 2.0 creates gatherings for those passionate about living with greater mindfulness, meaning, and wisdom in our modern age.

Loch Kelly

Loch Kelly is an author, meditation teacher, psychotherapist, and founder of the Open-Hearted Awareness Institute.

MrsMindfulness.com

Melli O'Brien is a meditation and mindfulness teacher who runs mindfulness retreats in Australia. Her guests are leading researchers, teachers and mindfulness experts who share their wisdom, knowledge, tips and tricks about mindfulness.

Podcasts

Ten Percent Happier, The Podcast

Yes, it's another *Ten Percent Happier* offering. **Dan Harris** talks with meditation pioneers, teachers, celebrities, scientists, and health experts about training our minds.

Tara Brach Podcast

Tara Brach combines her Ph.D. in Clinical Psychology with years of meditation practice to empower listeners to go deeper into their own practice. Her talks and guided meditations blend Western psychology and Eastern spiritual practices.

I Should Be Meditating Podcast

Adopting a daily practice of meditation takes passion and commitment, something that **Alan Kilma**, the host of *I Should Be Meditating*, knows all too well. Based on decades of experience, his talks and guided meditations can help you to be increasingly present in your life.

Books

For Skeptics

Ten Percent Happier: How I Tamed the Voice in My Head, Reduced Stress Without Losing My Edge, and Found Self-Help That Actually Works – A True Story by Dan Harris

The Mindful Geek: Mindfulness Meditation for Skeptics by Michael Taft

General

Full Catastrophe Living by Jon Kabat-Zinn

Wherever You Go There You Are by Jon Kabat-Zinn

Mindfulness in Plain English by Bhante Gunaratana

Business

Search Inside Yourself by Chad Meng Tan

Mindful Work by David Gelles

The Awakened Company by Catherine R. Bell

Children

Breathe and Be by Kate Coombs, Illustrated by Anna Laitinen

Websites

Jon Kabat-Zinn

https://www.mindfulnesscds.com/
Founder of Mindfulness-Based Stress Reduction (MBSR) and author of numerous books and CDs about mindfulness. You can find videos of his speeches, interviews and guided meditations on YouTube as well. His work is an excellent place to start learning about mindfulness and meditation.

Tara Brach

www.tarabrach.com

Founder of the Insight Meditation Community of Washington, DC. Her website is a wonderful resource for learning about meditation. You can learn about and order her books, there are guided meditations you can download and talks you can watch and download.

Jack Kornfield

www.jackkornfield.com

Cofounder of the Insight Meditation Society in Barre, MA and founder of Spirit Rock Center in Woodacre, CA. He is a Buddhist teacher and clinical psychologist, author of many books, articles and CDs. You can find written meditations, articles, and resources on his website. You can also find interviews with him on various podcasts in iTunes.

Daniel Siegel

www.drdansiegel.com

Founder of the Mindsight Institute, Dr. Siegel writes about mindfulness and Interpersonal Neurobiology as well as child development and parenting. You can find his books and other resources on his website.

The Basics of Mindfulness Practice

Mindfulness helps us put some space between ourselves and our reactions, breaking down our conditioned responses. Here's how to tune in to mindfulness throughout the day:

1. **Set aside some time.** You don't need a meditation cushion or bench, or any sort of special equipment to access your mindfulness skills—but you do need to set aside some time and space.

2. **Observe the present moment as it is.** The aim of mindfulness is not quieting the mind or attempting to achieve a state of eternal calm. The goal is simple: we're aiming to pay attention to the present moment, without judgment. Easier said than done, we know.

3. **Let your judgments roll by.** When we notice judgments arise during our practice, we can make a mental note of them and let them pass.

4. **Return to observing the present moment as it is.** Our minds often get carried away in thought. Mindfulness is the practice of returning, again and again, to the present moment.

5. **Be kind to your wandering mind.** Don't judge yourself for whatever thoughts crop up, just practice recognizing when your mind has wandered off and gently bring it back.

That's the practice. It's often been said that it's very simple, but not necessarily easy. The work is to just keep doing it. Results will accrue.

Sustaining a Meditation Practice

Start with Why: If you don't know why you want to meditate (i.e. how will it serve you? Improved relationships, reduced stress, being more present for your children) then it's going to be difficult to find the motivation to take the time out of your day to do it. Start with WHY.

Commit to a Set Period: You don't need to endeavor to meditate for the rest of your life. Allow that to unfold in its own time. For now, commit to something more short-term that feels realistic and attainable. Try 15 minutes a day for 30 days. Really commit to it. Whether you feel like meditating or not, just do it. Make it a habit like brushing your teeth.

One Minute Per Day: I suggest starting your first month with 15 minutes. However, if that feels like too much and you notice yourself slipping, commit to just one minute. Everyone has one minute, and it's hard to argue yourself out of it. However, once most people begin, they sit for longer.

Meditation Buddy: Accountability is huge when it comes to starting a new habit. Find a friend or family member interested in meditating or starting a new habit, and text each other each day to make sure you both follow through.

ACKNOWLEDGEMENTS

To begin, I want to thank Dr. Stephen Johnson, my former therapist and author of *The Sacred Path: The Way of the Spiritual Warrior*. Ironically, when I needed it the most, my cynicism about meditation was at an all-time high. Without his guidance and persistence, I would never have grabbed what turned out be my life preserver. It was Dr. Johnson who threw it to me.

I'd also like to thank another spiritual warrior, former Coast Guard Commander and Police Lieutenant, Richard Goerling of Mindful Badge. My work teaching federal and local law enforcement personnel was greatly informed by Richard's Mindfulness Based Resiliency Training (MBRT). From the moment I spied him on the cover of Mindful Magazine, in full police uniform and a half lotus position, I knew I had to work with him; a spiritual warrior indeed.

I have had too many brilliant meditation teachers to give them all their due, so I will briefly name a few of them and with some words as to how they influenced my journey. In order of their influence on me they are: Jon Kabat-Zinn, the father of secular mindfulness, whose seminal book Dr. Johnson insisted I read; Brian Shiers, the gentleman who's six week course inspired me to teach mindful meditation; Diana Winston, the inspiring Director of the Mindful Awareness Research Center at UCLA; Fleet Maull, PhD, criminal justice mindful pioneer and founder of the Engaged Mindfulness Institute.

On a more personal note, I want to thank my departed loving parents, Julian S. Stein and Lucy Morehead Reynolds. Dad for his tireless optimism and unconditional love, and mom for her deep intellectual curiosity and astonishing wisdom. I also want to thank them for providing me with a big, noisy and fabulous family.

Closer to home, I couldn't have psychologically endured writing this book without the unwavering support of my long-suffering wife, the gorgeous and learned, Susan McGuire. Both of us show business survivors, today she's a successful Marriage and Family Therapist (MFT) and Jungian Analyst. I also want to recognize my brilliant niece, Allison McGuire, for her always savvy support and unconditional love.

I want to make a shout out to my sister, Denny Stein, for her readings of my earliest chapters, assuring me they, "weren't too bad." This alone gave me the burst of confidence I needed to keep going. In the latter part of the process, my intrepid proof-reader, Sheila Hall, cleaned up my grammatical messes and editorially took a machete to everything that needed to go.

Last but not least, I am so thankful to my fearless editor and publisher, Valerie Alexander. After hearing a talk I gave and watching me teach, she persuaded me to do the impossible: to actually write a book! She talked me into it and played me like a violin; offering great notes, supplying needed encouragement and demonstrating endless patience. I am exceedingly proud to be part of her, "…. as a Second Language," series.

And finally, to you the reader, it is my fervent hope that the information in these pages will have you seriously consider starting, maintaining, nurturing and investing in your own daily (or near daily) meditation practice. If you do, my work is complete.

ABOUT THE AUTHORS

Nick Stein

Before mindfulness came into his life, Nick Stein had been a hard charging non-fiction TV cameraman, editor, director, producer and show runner across a forty-year career in television. In that time, he created scores of documentaries for all four broadcast networks, as well as the most watched cable channels, including Discovery, History, A&E, Smithsonian and National Geographic.

From 2009 to 2012, Nick produced National Geographic Channel's hit series *Border Wars,* as he and his crews gained unparalleled access to law enforcement units patrolling the contested areas of the U.S.-Mexico border. An instant success, *Border Wars* came out as the highest rated premiere in the 25-year history of the channel and went on to become Nat Geo's highest rated prime time series for some time.

However, Nick's four years of bearing witness to tragic levels of human suffering at the border – on both sides of the badge – led him to a bad case of burnout. Being away from home for so long also caused stress on his marriage and personal life. Seeking relief from this unhappy state, Nick discovered a secular and science-based form of meditation called mindfulness while working in Montreal, Canada. It was then that he began his journey from novice meditator to professional teacher.

Returning home to Los Angeles, Nick began a rigorous training regimen at UCLA's Mindful Awareness Research Center (MARC). After two years in their Intensive Practice Program (IPP), Nick was accepted into the inaugural class of the Engaged Mindfulness Institute (EMI) in Massachusetts and received a Certification of Mindfulness Facilitation in June 2016. Shortly after that he was accepted into the International Mindfulness Teachers Association (IMTA).

Since then, Nick has brought his unique style of teaching to a variety of populations and institutions. Using his strong communications background, Nick helps people initiate and maintain a meditation practice by emphasizing its logical, practical and learnable nature. He calls his approach *Strategic Stillness* and under that banner he shares his hard-won knowledge with CEOs and key executives in a multiplicity of industries. You can find Nick working on college campuses, at high tech startups and at meditation centers throughout Los Angeles. He also donates his time in pro-bono work, in one case spending a year bringing mindfulness to prisoners inside the notorious L.A. County Men's Jail.

With all this, Nick is perhaps best known for his work with law enforcement. After his immersion in police culture through the making of Border Wars, Nick was among the very first mindfulness instructors to work with U.S. Customs and Border Protection (CBP) Border Patrol Agents and Land Port Officers. He's also worked with local police agencies from coast to coast. From chiefs and supervisors to captains, detectives and patrol officers, Nick helps these frontline men and women foster compassion and resilience as they cope, shift after shift and year after year, with some of the most tragic of society's problems. With Nick's help they discover that mindful meditation can lead to stronger social connections, better focus, and a greater sense of well-being and purpose, all viable tools for self-regulation and stress reduction.

Nick resides in Southern California his wife, Susan.

You can reach Nick through his website,
StrategicStillness.com

Valerie Alexander

Valerie Alexander is a renowned expert on happiness and inclusion, and a globally-recognized speaker on the topics of happiness in the workplace, the advancement of women, and unconscious bias.

Valerie's TED Talk, "How to Outsmart Your Own Unconscious Bias" is one of the most viewed on the topic, and she has spoken at hundreds of conferences, colleges and companies around the world. She was also the commencement speaker for her undergraduate alma mater, Trinity University, giving the inspiring talk, "Tiger at Heart."

Valerie owns the U.S. Registered Trademark on the phrase, "…as a Second Language" for books in the self-help, personal growth, motivation and self-esteem categories. Her books include:

- *Happiness as a Second Language,* an Amazon #1 Seller
- *Success as a Second Language*
- *How Women Can Succeed in the Workplace (Despite Having "Female Brains"),*

plus several more she's published in the trademarked series.

As a screenwriter, Valerie worked with Joel Schumacher, Catherine Zeta Jones, Ice Cube and others. She has written, produced and directed more than 50 commercials, short films and public service announcements, including the award winning, "*Ballpark Bullies,*" and the groundbreaking commercials, "*Say I Do,*" "*Life Support*" and "*The Wedding*

Matters," in support of everyone's freedom to marry. She also writes movies for the Hallmark Channel, including "*Memories of Christmas*" starring Christina Milian, ranked by Good Housekeeping as the #9 Best Hallmark Christmas Movies of all time and by Parade as the #25 Best Hallmark Christmas Movie of all time.

Valerie started her career in the Silicon Valley as a securities lawyer, an investment banker, and an Internet executive, working on some of the biggest transactions of the Internet era, before transitioning into the entertainment industry. From 2016 – 2019, she returned to her corporate roots as the founder and CEO of Goalkeeper, a tech startup that built communication platforms that made it easier for you to make the people you love happy.

Valerie received her B.A. from Trinity, her M.S. in environmental economics from U.C., Berkeley, and her J.D. from Berkeley Law, where she was invited back to teach the legal ethics course, "Representation of Law in Film." She also holds a certification in the Science of Happiness from the Greater Good Science Center at U.C., Berkeley.

Valerie lives in Los Angeles with her husband and their ill-mannered German Shepherd, Vegas, Baby!

You can reach Valerie through her website,
SpeakHappiness.com

Other Books in the "...as a Second Language" series